30 PASSIVE INCOME IDEAS

"I believe that Darryl is a human locksmith, he knows how to open your mind to larger possibilities and make you see FURTHER than you did before. Using his unique insights into human nature, he's found a way to simplify the passive income strategies of the skilled passive income earners so that anyone can have the financial freedom they deserve."

- **Sir Terence Wallen**

30 PASSIVE INCOME IDEAS

THE MOST TRUSTED PASSIVE INCOME GUIDE TO TAKING CHARGE & BUILDING YOUR RESIDUAL INCOME PORTFOLIO

DARRYL JAMES

DMJ Publishing

30 PASSIVE INCOME IDEAS (3rd Edition)
THE MOST TRUSTED PASSIVE INCOME GUIDE TO TAKING CHARGE & BUILDING YOUR RESIDUAL INCOME PORTFOLIO

© 2020 by **DARRYL JAMES. DMJ PUBLISHING.**

Published in Birmingham, England by DMJ Publishing.
www.dmjpublishing.co.uk

ISBN
9798645340384

Cover Design by
Scale DM

Illustrations
Canva Pro

DMJ Publishing

Disclaimer Notice:

Table Of Contents

Foreword

The Private Eye of Profit

Back in the 1930s the word 'eye' was first used in this connection. The 'eye' was in fact 'I' as an abbreviation for – investigator.

And now, there's **Darryl James.**

The Private Eye of Profit – seeking out the little know ways and means, methods and systems, techniques and tips to gather a handsome return from our entrepreneurial adventures.

Over the course of this book, he uncovers, examines and gives us the dirt on 30 (Yes, 30) proven methods of making passive income. Of course, like any 'passive income', there's work to be done at the start.

"In the beginning you do a lot of work you don't get paid for, so that in the future you get paid for a lot of work you no longer have to do"

From car wraps (yes, seriously) to recruiting; from swipes for partners, even Apps to book publishing – Darryl not only give you the what, he explains the when, the where – and the all-important 'how'.

Join him now on your personal journey of discovery ready to grasp which idea (or ideas) match with you, your style and your goals – and enjoy even more – passive income...

Peter Thomson
"The World's Most Prolific Information Product Creator"

Introduction

"Create your vision and start living the life of your dreams"
Darryl James

How would you live your life if you could wake up each morning knowing there was enough money coming into your bank account that month, to cover not only your bills and expenses but also for you to go on holiday and live the life you always wanted?

Many of you would keep working because that is the way we were taught. Even if you had a choice, you would probably choose to keep on working and work from a place of joy and abundance. You would work because you wanted to, not because you **had to,** and the rat race would end.

Ever since I was in my mid-twenties, I've been determined to have my own business and to build enough passive income in order not to have to work at a job. A future that included getting into the office by 8 a.m. and leaving well after 8 p.m. each day for decades seemed too brutal to endure.

5

Looking back over the last ten years, it seems that destiny played a significant role in the unfolding of events that led to me becoming an author on passive income.

When writing this third edition I took a look at the feedback and the questions I was receiving in the group, and have addressed these accordingly. I also have more to say with new experiences, new wisdom and new knowledge in each area.

Why a third edition? - I wanted to make sure that as I was growing in knowledge, I was giving continual value to my readers. My life experiences have significantly developed since the first edition of this book. By meeting more experts and entrepreneurs like myself, I have gleaned and gained more wisdom that I wish to share with my readers.

Since the first version of 30 Passive Income Ideas, I had people from as young as 12 and as old as 69 tell me how much my words have inspired them and financially improved their life.

I am both humbled and excited to be writing a new edition of this book, as I have had a variety of jobs in many industries over my adult life. I have been a Music Artist/Producer, Secondary School Teacher, Marketing Director, Record Label owner and started many businesses in a variety of fields, mainly online. While navigating somewhat all over the place, I always put 100% effort into what I was doing and whom I was becoming. I say somewhat all over the place, as I often had "shiny penny syndrome" - shiny penny syndrome is when you see something with potential and then go for it. Although brave, this can also be detrimental to your health and state of mind if these shiny pennies don't accumulate into pounds and notes after the effort and long hours. Although I was successful in many of my jobs, businesses, and ventures, I also failed in many. I felt lost, frustrated, confused and as though I was wandering into the abyss at times. I remember days and weeks where I would be chasing clients for the money that they owed me and worried about paying bills and the rent on my new home. Relationships with loved ones, often suffered too, as I worked tirelessly and sometimes had too much determination.

Why am I telling you this? I am telling you this because, after over 15 years of working harder than many of my peers and mentors; I decided I need more time, freedom, and that I want my money to work hard for me instead of me merely working hard for my money.

I wanted to have more time to look after and be with loved ones, to travel, to see the world other than by travelling to business or industry conventions. I needed more time to have fun and live my life in an amazing and fulfilled way. I had tunnel vision and used to have years pass me by without noticing that people were getting older and I had not been living life at all. I remember I was jumping from one thing to another, focusing on so many things at the same time and thinking "why isn't this working the way I want it to?" I either had money and no time or time and no money. I would often catch myself thinking "I deserve this, people that are successful, are not working harder than me, not 10 x smarter than me, yet they are better than me and have the freedom to do as they like". So, if we all put on our trousers in the morning one leg at a time, then there must be something I am missing. I then focused heavily on self-development by reading books and taking courses from the likes of Robert Kiyosaki, Tony Robbins, T.Harv Ecker, Jim Rohn, Zig Ziglar and many others.

Nonetheless, studying Self-development had its good points and bad points. I would change like the wind on which author was the best, which strategy and industry were the best, and finally, I decided to go with my passion - which is writing and creating. I looked at things from a different perspective, and for me, the race was over.

The choice had to be made. Move over to the passive income side, or stay in the paid hourly side where I'm unhappy with the amount of time I'm grafting (I believe in working hard, just for something you love and enjoy) and not see any results. There must be another way, right? Enter Passive Income!

This book isn't just about passive income; it is about making the transition to passive income streams, to financial freedom, and creating the life that you desire.

I am the relentless guy that watches Dragons Den, Shark Tank, The Profit, and The Apprentice UK, longing to be better, to grow and gain wisdom in this rollercoaster world that we live in. Although I enjoyed the ideas and business acumen, if I were to unlock my deepest desires and fulfil my dreams (like you will too) I needed to be honest with myself and ask myself three vital questions:

1. Where am I?
2. Where do I want to go?
3. How am I going to get there?

The answers to these questions will give you the foundation of what you need to know in order to take advantage of any opportunity.

I have been looking into passive/residual income for many years and decided to create the third edition of this book, highlighting some of the passive income ideas that worked for me and also some of the ideas & strategies that worked for my diverse network of close friends.

When I began writing this book, I did not just rely on my own experience I also drew from my friends' and associates' lessons on passive income. I sat closely, observed, conducted case studies and interviewed many entrepreneurs, especially those that are financially free and have the money and time to live life on their own terms. Some of these interviews can be found on my Podcast show "Business Marketing Finance" which is available on Apple Podcasts, Spotify Podcasts and about 8 other platforms.

What You Will Learn in This Book
My mentor always told me that:
"Risk comes from not knowing what you are doing."

Warren Buffet

I want to accelerate your learning curve in terms of what opportunities are available to you in the fantastic world of passive income - both online and offline.

I have researched and looked into the best passive income opportunities and these 30 residual income ideas are so simple that anybody can do them. Some will require new skills, saving for the initial investment, hiring another person and joint ventures, but anybody with the dedication to their goals can achieve any one of them. This book has captured all of these ideas in one place to save you time so that you can compare and see which one is best for you.

95% of the world live life the linear and traditional way. They do what is normal around them. They go to school, go to college, get a job, retire at 65 and then die. Most people fail to actually live their lives, and what is worse is that the moment they stop working they cannot pay their bills.

College/University vs. the New Model
Passive income can be hard to get. Just because it is passive, it doesn't mean that it is easy. Now, why do people only know how to produce active or linear income? The number one reason is that we were taught this from a young age, and our environment was more than likely one where our parents did and were taught the same. Now school sets you up for learning, but it also sets you up to be an employee, in the school system we

are only taught linear income. There is no "how to follow your passion class", "how to leverage class", teachings about your credit score or a passive income class. If there were, I would've taken them. My team and I will be combating this as we believe like many others that the next generation needs to know these things as well as countless other life skills. Be sure to look out for this on www.businessmarketingfinance.com; it's going to be HUGE!

If, like me, you want more time, more opportunities and more choices in life, then this book is for you. If you are crazy enough to prefer the mundane, lack of free time and continuously being told when to wake up, when to eat and in some cases even when to go to the toilet, then kindly pass this book on to someone who may benefit from it, as this book is not for you.

Wouldn't it be great to retire by 30? By 40 or 50 years of age instead of the national average of 65?

Task

Take a few minutes before you start to read the chapters in this book to answer the following four questions:

1. Why do you want to earn passive income?
2. How much passive income will it take for you to become financially free? (Remember this means enough money coming in passively that covers all of your expenses)

3. What would you do with your time if you did not have to work?
4. How much money would you LOVE to earn passively?

If you are ready for a different life and to actually LIVE life, then continue reading, you will be blown away by how accessible some of these tools are to you.

Why you will come back to this book again and again

While sharing all the updates and new strategies for my 30 Passive Income Ideas third edition, I also needed to answer the question "What happens when my expenses grow far more than my passive income". An example of this could be starting a family and having twins, or unresolved debt coming to bite you in the ass or a loved one becoming ill, and you are now a carer, and therefore your expenses have now grown past the passive income streams you had coming in.

I remember some years ago how I thought I was free, safe and had enough money covering my expenses not to have to work. I soon encountered a milestone that meant I needed to go back to work for a year until some debts were paid off or I raised my monthly passive income even higher to accommodate the new expenses. Thankfully this only lasted a year, and I was happy to be financially free again. That experience taught me a lesson that I needed to add in this book.

Just because you are free doesn't mean you will be free forever. You may find yourself using any number of these streams to earn passive income. So that's the key – don't aim for financial freedom aim for economic confidence in where you learn the strategies to be paid forever on something and diversify your portfolio. Once you have one, then try another and another - aim to have a passive income **portfolio**. That will make you financially free for LIFE! That is true freedom, where you're not depending on having to go back to work, Google or Facebook ads or your social media following. You make your money, but you only focus on passive income.

You will have multiple streams of income passively. This book will show you the skills that you need and not just passive income titles/ideas. You can read a blog for that.

The 4 types of income:

Leverage Income

Leveraged income means you are now leveraging other people's time, other people's talents and other people's resources. Leveraging other people means you have a business or system in place so that you are no longer relying on your own time and resources.

Linear/Active Income

Linear and active income mean that for every hour you work, you get paid for that hour. You are trading hours for pounds. With 24hours in each day, you are then limited to how much you can earn with your active hours of the day (not sleeping).

Windfall Income

Windfall Income is a sudden, unexpected profit or gain. A windfall may occur, for example, from selling a business, selling stocks after making a profit, an inheritance or even winning the lottery.

Passive Income

Then there is Passive Income (also known as residual income):

What is Passive Income?

Simply put, passive income is the income you receive on a recurring basis after doing something upfront only once. In other words, you do something once but get paid forever.

Passive income (also called residual, or recurring income) is income that continues to be generated after the initial effort has been expended. Compare this to what most people focus on earning: linear income, which is "one-shot" compensation or payment in the form of a fee, wage, commission or salary. –

Oxford Dictionary.

The beautiful thing about passive income is that once you set it up, you can earn it while you are sleeping, on holiday or playing with your kids on a sunny afternoon.

Passive income comes from assets you have, and assets are either bought with money (e.g., currency, rental property) or in the case of most of the ideas in this book, they are acquired through sweat and work upfront, for example, music royalties, after releasing a song or the writing and self-publishing of a book. **This book is not a get rich quick book**. I believe you have to work hard in anything for it to be a success. It may take a while for passive income to become a stream for you. Keep persevering and know that eventually those drips will become a stream and in some cases flow into a river. Building a passive/residual income portfolio and having multiple income streams allows you to work hard once, then see the fruit of your labour without planting the seed again and again.

All these passive income streams require at least one of the following elements:

1. An upfront monetary investment
2. An upfront time investment

You cannot earn residual income without being willing to provide at least one of these two.

Please don't be the shiny-object type of person. Stop chasing everything that comes your way. Be truthful with yourself in the tools you need and the people you have around you. It may feel productive but it's not, and you will build many houses and finish none.

The Acorn

In this game, you have to have a depth of field, to see beyond what is in focus. Think long term. With a depth of field in mind, close your eyes for 1 minute, and picture an acorn.

What do you see?

Many people will say they see a tree from where the acorn fell from, themselves holding an acorn or just a forest where the acorn lay after it landed.
I'll tell you what I see. I see the same tree, but I then see the forest, that the tree came from, I then see the multitude of houses built from the wood from those trees. I then take it further, and I see a city and the communities built from those houses. I then see a civilization and great masses of people living their dreams and contributing to society. I see this, all from just one acorn.
The goal of this book is to help you take calculated risks. So that you stop trading precious time for money and live a life of freedom.

It can be incredibly tempting to pick out three or more passive income ideas to get started with, but I would encourage you to pick one in the beginning. You need time and the ability to focus on cultivating and growing a passive income stream. You must master one thing before moving on to another.

It is going to take a substantial amount of time and/or money in the beginning but earning passive income is the best thing that can happen to you.

Choose an idea, make a plan, and dedicate yourself to it until that income stream comes to fruition.

I desire that you genuinely connect with this book and that it ignites you and gives you new viewpoints, as new viewpoints position us for new insights and new insights help us move past our current limitations.

Your Self-Image

I think it is important to dedicate a chapter to the topics of mindset and self-image.

What you believe about yourself, you will allow to flow or cease. The gap between knowing what you need to do and actually doing is only bridged by an obsessive desire for change.

If you find yourself procrastinating and not getting things done, it is simply because deep down inside, you feel that you do not have to or somehow don't deserve what you desire. Subconsciously you are comfortable with where you are right now and changing your routine is too uncomfortable. The change will only come once you are convinced that staying in your current situation/routine is uncomfortable and unacceptable. Unfortunately, most people have to hit rock bottom before this change occurs.

Example - You want to lose weight for a friend's wedding that is happening in 6 months' time, let's say 20lbs. No matter what diet or exercise plan you follow, if you even finish that diet or plan you will return to your original weight very quickly, unless you see yourself as being healthier, stronger, fitter and without the weight.
The human brain likes to prove itself right, so you will mess up on your diet again and again, or get lazy the odd day here and there, and you will not exercise.

Still not convinced? Here's another example:

Let's say you really want to move up the ladder in the organisation that you work for. If you do not see yourself as being able to do it, you will subconsciously not make all the efforts to add value to your organisation for them to promote you. You will allow colleagues and gossip to sway you from your goals. You will have a track record of being tardy, or not go the extra mile on a project or task, thus you fail to increase your value in order to get a new position. You subconsciously believe you would not get it anyway.

18

Growing up, I struggled with my self-image. Coming from a single parent home in a rough neighborhood without my father or a strong male figure around, I began looking to my family and peers to show or explain to me what life and money were about. The only problem was that they were finding their way in pretty much the same environment as I was, and they didn't have much either. Eventually, some of their limited views were passed down to me. I grew up believing some incorrect statements about money. I had to take charge and look deep within! I encourage you to do so also:

Discover your current beliefs about money – What thoughts occur in your mind due to conditioning, that you currently agree with?

Have a look at this list and see if any of these limiting statements resonate with you.

- "I am not worthy of money."
- "Money is extremely hard to get."
- "When it rains it pours."
- "Ahhhh, I always get bad luck."
- "Some people have all the luck."
- "That's good for them I am proud of them, but I could never do that."
- "I will have to work really hard if I want to become rich and will risk losing friends and my current lifestyle."
- "More money, more problems."
- "Money is the root of all evil."
- "There is not enough to go around."

- "If I have money, I am depriving someone else of having money."
- "I do not deserve to have wealth."
- "I need money to make money."
- "It is not fair for me to have money if someone else doesn't."

If you have been totally honest with yourself, you would've probably noticed that you hold some crushing belief systems about money. Did you see that hidden deep within your thought processes money is somehow connected to pain, scarcity, lack, hard work, struggle, greed, corruption or inequality?

Can you see there may be some conflict between your values – and your pursuit of money?

These statements are harmful to your thinking, and you are subconsciously holding yourself back from opportunities.

What We Believe - We Attract.

Our subtle belief systems affect everything in our lives. Some people believe they are not worthy of health. Other people feel they're not worthy of love. Others think they must do what they hate in order to earn a living, and some people would like to move to a new area or even relocate to another country, yet believe they can never move from where they are.

There is an old saying:

"Whether you believe you can, or you believe you cannot – you are right!"

Henry Ford

Our practical life experience is primarily influenced by these subconscious and unconscious beliefs (or Inner Self Image). If we want something to change in our lives, we need to uncover these underlying old belief systems and exchange them with new ones. You cannot change the past, but you can change your devaluing attitude and weak thoughts starting right now. These subtle inner shifts have profound and noticeable effects on your life. Every thought counts, and you can begin NOW to make changes for the better. Wherever or whoever you are, no matter what you have experienced in the past, you can change your thought patterns and attitude.

The old pattern:
Money = pain, struggle, hard work, corruption, evil, hard to get, scarce

The new pattern:
Money = joy, fulfillment, free time, helping others, freedom, feeling alive.
The more you reinforce this new association, the faster the old belief systems will be replaced with money

attracting systems, and that is what the Foundation to wealth is all about.

When you become financially free, you may learn that free time isn't what you truly desire. However, you desire to be able to do what retired people do, but you need to live your passion. I'm a visionary and creative individual, so for me that passion is business, videos, and making music. I LOVE music. So now that is what I do, but if I want to take some time out or to study something entirely new, I can do so without fear, obligation or worry about how I will be able to feed myself or my family.

How to afford your initial passive income investment?

Save until it hurts each month. Most people think they are saving enough through their pension or savings account, but they are not. Developing passive income requires an aggressive after tax and savings amount to be invested each month. I usually advise my clients to save at least 10% of their income for their financial freedom fund. I also recommend this to you. Set up a new bank account for this, arrange it so that as soon as your wage goes into your bank account, it is deposited into your financial freedom account so that you don't even see the money. The money is taken out automatically each payday.

It would be best if you sacrificed the pleasures of today for the freedom you will earn tomorrow. This may mean no holidays for a year or two, buying non-branded clothes or not upgrading your car until you've saved up enough cash for your investment.

Calculate how much passive income you need. It's essential to have a number and a passive-income goal if you like, otherwise, it's very easy to lose motivation. A good goal is to try to generate enough passive income to cover necessary living expenses such as food, home/shelter, transportation, and clothing.

Now with that being said. Let's get started!

Your FREE Gift (£29.99 Value)

As a way of saying thank you for your purchase, I'm offering for free my "How to find your niche" quick start guide as well as my "66 ways to market any product or service" cheat sheet.

With this "How to Find Your Niche" guide you will be able to understand what a niche is, see examples of niches/sub-niches and easily be able to pick YOUR niche within Drop shipping, YouTube, Blogging, Affiliate Marketing and many more of the passive income ideas in the following chapters. Everything you need to get started, you can implement them in your chosen strategy and have 66 ways you can market your chosen idea.

Grab the How to Find Your Niche quick start guide and 66 Ways to Market Your Product or Service cheat sheet here: **www.businessmarketingfinance.com/readers**

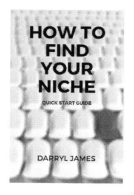

30 PASSIVE INCOME IDEAS

"Money is a good servant but a bad master."

— SIR FRANCIS BACON

T-shirt Mastery

A close friend of mine makes a good amount of recurring income (Avg £3400 PCM) using this passive income stream. Creating the design for T-shirts and then selling them on sites such as Merch by Amazon, CaféPress and also Teespring. These websites allow you to sell high-quality t-shirts perfectly tailored to your audience, with ZERO upfront cost.

Once you have picked your niche, choose any of the above platforms, design and upload your artwork, choose a T-shirt type and colour, set your price, and add a product description. Merch by Amazon, CaféPress or Teespring will then create a product page on their platform. When a customer buys your t-shirt, they'll handle production, shipping, packing, and the customer service for you. The best thing is that you name the price, so each time you make a sale, Amazon, Teespring, or CafePress (All three platforms if you desire) will print the item, ship it to your buyers, and then you split the profits. If your t-shirt design becomes popular and makes sales, you'll be able to earn an income on your T-shirt design for life.

If you choose to use Merch by Amazon, your T-shirt designs are also eligible for Prime users, which is a massive bonus, as many people opt for prime over standard sellers when purchasing, as it provides not only a faster delivery option but adds credibility to the product.

Selling T-shirts is an excellent way to make passive income if you are an illustrator or designer or just good with a pencil. If you have no technical skills but have a good eye for design, using Merch by Amazon and Teespring's easy online design creators you can create your T-shirt design quite simply in just a few minutes.

Teespring & CafePress also allow you to add your designs on a variety of other items such as Mugs, Leggings, Gym Vests, Hoodies, T-shirts (Men's & Women's), Baby clothes and much more.

Many people look for unique gifts on Amazon, CafePress and Teespring. Every Holiday there are tens of thousands of people buying novelty gear from Halloween, Christmas and Computer Nerd T-shirts, Mugs and Hoodies. Catchphrases such as "You are what you eat" for vegans and quotes such as "The journey of a thousand miles, begins with a first step" for entrepreneurs. However, it doesn't stop with just novelty gear; a simple but efficient way is to use Google to search for motivational quotes (or use Instagram to find them), then redesign the same quote and upload the design to Merch by Amazon, CafePress or Teespring.

More on CafePress later, however, the main advantage of using companies like Amazon and Teespring is that you don't have to stock any of the products, buy bulk equipment or print anything yourself. Your job is only to come up with great designs and leveraging their platforms, let these giants do the work for you.

If you would like to sell T-shirts on your website or platform, then I recommend Shopify.

Shopify is an all in one e-commerce solution that is very easy to use and has excellent support if you have any setup or general running issues.

Once you have set up your Shopify store using one of their many free themes, then you can use an app such as Printful to fulfill orders.

Printful is easy to use:

When an order is made on Shopify (or even eBay) with a Printful product, the order is directly sent to Printful (offices in America & Europe), where they will print and ship it to your customer under your brand.
Integrating Printful with your Shopify store is easy:

1. Create your Printful and Shopify accounts,

2. Click the "Get" button on the Printful app page and follow the instructions,
3. Upload designs and sync existing products that you'd like to fulfill through them, or easily create new ones with their product generator,
4. Set up your billing and shipping, and you're done!

With Printful, you get:

- Control over your profit: They charge you the bare minimum to cover production - you set your end price, and what's left is your profit
- Discounted samples: Order product samples with 20% off + free shipping.
- Free mockups: Create product mockups with their mock-up generator.
- White label: You won't see Printful on any of your orders, you can use your own logo and branding.
- Stress-free shipping: Lost/damaged shipments are on them, and domestic orders come with a tracking code.
- Warehousing & Fulfillment: Store your entire inventory at their warehouse, and they'll fulfill all your orders.

Hot Tips:

1. You can also outsource design work to websites such as www.scaledm.co.uk, www.dribble.co/, and www.fiverr.com if you don't want to create the designs yourself.

2. Canva is another great place to start if you are not a designer. Canva is a graphic design platform that allows users to create social media graphics, presentations, posters and other visual content. It is available on web and mobile devices, and integrates millions of images, fonts, templates and illustrations. Canva has many templates for you to choose from and even a category dedicated to just T-shirt templates. The process is fairly easy as they give you the templates to edit so you will already have the right font and graphics, ready and waiting.

3. Promote, promote, promote! It goes without saying that most ventures these days should have a social media and online presence to engage with your consumers. While you are posting your latest designs to your followers on Facebook, Instagram and even LinkedIn in some cases, why not run some targeted Facebook and Instagram ads to drive sales even further!

"Entrepreneurship is living a few years of your life like most people won't so you can spend the rest of your life like most people can't."

- Warren G. Tracy

Book Publishing Empire

Self-publishing is very popular these days. When you buy a paperback book or an eBook off of Amazon, there's a pretty good chance you're buying a self-published book. Self-publishing has become very accessible to anyone. I tried this a few years ago and when I published the first edition of my book, I couldn't believe how simple the process was. Helping 6 authors in just a short few years, I published 8 books through my book publishing company DMJ Publishing, using the methods I am about to teach you.

To self-publish an eBook or book, you'll first need to write and edit it, create a cover, and then upload these files to a platform such as Amazon's Kindle Direct Publishing (KDP) to get your new book into stores.

The success of your eBook/Book will primarily be a result of the following:
- How good was your headline?

- How helpful was the targeted information to your audience?
- Did you use a book funnel?

A book funnel can be a potent selling tool. A funnel is a marketing system. It's the "ideal" process you intend your customers to experience as they go from prospect to lead to customer to repeat buyer.

With a book funnel, you can offer your book at a limited time discounted offer rate, and when people purchase your book, they can receive a one-time offer for step by step training or additional resources (also known as upselling).

After you write your eBook, you could easily create that eBook into an audiobook using ACX which is Amazons Audiobook platform. You then have two choices you can either produce the audiobook yourself using a relatively cheap podcast microphone (Rode NT1A is a good start for around £90), and software such as GarageBand or Soundforge, or you can hire a producer to do the whole thing for you from recording to editing to the final piece. You can either pay them a flat fee (between £50-£200 per finished hour) and/or a royalty from the proceeds of the audiobook. Audible will then add it to their marketplace as well as iTunes. Your audiobook will also appear as an option to purchase on your Amazon listings page for your eBook and/or paperback versions.

There are several places you can publish your book including Amazon's Kindle Direct Publishing, Google Play, Barnes & Noble and Lulu. The essential services on these publishing sites are free, and you can pay for premium services like sponsored ads, marketing and editing from them if needs be.

If you are a writer, storyteller or like to talk about the things you enjoy and have a lot of knowledge about a particular topic, you can write a 60-120 page eBook (average length) and sell it through Amazon KDP, Google Play, iBook's (Apple), Nook (Barnes and Noble) or Kobo. It would be best if you had your presence on multiple channels such as the ones above, because multi-channels equal maximum exposure, and that is key to dominating in this business.

Topic

You can research what is hot right now by using google trends or by visiting the Amazon book section and browsing the headings and subheadings of popular book titles. Your core topic should be well thought out and focused on a niche.

Special Bonus

Have you downloaded your FREE (£29.99 Value) bonuses yet? This includes a special PDF guide about niches. If not head over to:
www.businessmarketingfinance.com/readers

Content

Although writing your first book can be quite daunting, the average e-book is only 10,000 words long. Just planning on writing 500 words a day means that you could finish the content of your book in just three weeks! When picking a subject, it is important to note, that you should choose a topic that you know a lot of information about already. People are far more likely to buy and read a book from someone they perceive to be an authority than from someone who has no authority at all.

Editing

Editing ensures your book is error-free and impactful, with flawless language and formatting. A good editor should also give you objective feedback on the arguments, organisation, tone, and more. I recommend doing some research on the best editors online. These days I like to use my editor at DMJ Publishing (in house team) however you can use editors from www.thecreativepenn.com/editors.
I used some of these editors in the past and they are very good.

Book Cover

Canva, mentioned in the previous chapter, is a good place to start if you have no idea what your front cover should look like. Canva has many templates for you to choose from and even a category dedicated to just book cover templates. Go to https://Canva.com to access the free version of their site although I recommend paying for the pro version at $12.99 pcm.

Formatting

Once your e-book/book is written, edited and designed, the final step is to format your book. I recommend following the instructions outlined by Amazon which can be found here: https://kdp.amazon.com/en_US/help/topic/A17W8UM0M MSQX6

Ads

You can advertise your new book using sponsored ads through Amazon. Sponsored ads allow you to reach Amazon customers as they research and discover products. The keywords you set up, allow Ads to appear on search results pages and relevant product pages, directing customers to your book's details page.
Be sure to use your mailing lists and social media (Facebook, Twitter, Instagram), guest posting, Click Bank and bloggers to get potential buyers' attention and get them to purchase your book.

One of the great things about writing a book/eBook is that most of the online bookstores such as Amazon and iBook's list and sell your eBook on their platforms for you with no upfront fees. You only have to pay a commission (30%) to them every time your eBook sells.
Amazon KDP will rank you higher if you have a three-month exclusivity with them. One way to combat this is to reskin your eBook as a "special Kindle edition" and still release the eBook on all the other platforms if you so wish.

If you want to make a lot of money from your eBook, then it's all about selling it to your friends, family, associates, social followers and getting bloggers and email marketers to affiliate sale for you like crazy. Affiliate sales are the latest big thing (more on this later), and I have seen first-hand how well it works.

Whether you connect with affiliates one by one or list your products on affiliate marketplaces such as Click bank and Amazon affiliates, the best way is directly connecting with as many people as possible, giving them everything they need to sell and duplicate the process. Duplication is key.

Hot Tips:

1. When writing your description for your book. If you are not familiar with HTML, use an editor such as https://kindlepreneur.com/amazon-book-description-generator/ as this will help your book stand out.

2. Information about pricing your e-book: https://kdp.amazon.com/help?topicId=A3KL1PS54 8IZK2

3. Besides. having a Book/eBook you can also have a narrated version in the form of an audio book and sell on sites such as Amazon Audible or have advertisers pay you to be in the intro and outro of your Audiobook with sites such as www.thecreativepenn.com

Here are some useful terms if you are producing your audiobook yourself:

Useful Terms

Artifact: Undesirable sounds around words, such as random, humming noises and metallic sounding breaths. Artifacts can be added to the original audio from excessive or incorrect noise reduction resulting from technical limitations.

Attack Time: The amount of time it takes for a dynamics processor to begin adjusting gain once the signal exceeds the threshold setting.

Attenuate: To reduce in force or make quieter.

Bandwidth: A measure of a range of frequencies in Hertz (Hz), or musical octaves. **See "Q" also**.

Boost: To increase, raise or make louder.

Brickwall Limiting: A type of hard limiting that causes a full square wave effect. **See "Limiting" also**.

Clipping: Also called "Digital Clipping", clipping occurs when a digital signal peak reaches or rises above 0dBFS (Decibels Full Scale). This is often interpreted as an undesirable distorted sound, and should always be avoided. To avoid clipping, reduce the signal's input before the gain stage in which the clipping occurs.

Compressor: A dynamics processor that is used to narrow an audio signal's overall dynamic range by reducing the volume of loud portions, while amplifying the quiet portions. Adjustable parameters generally include attack, release, threshold, and make-up gain.

Constant Bitrate (CBR): An encoding standard for audio files that forces all of a codec's output data to be uniform.

Cut: Remove a portion of audio.

Digital Audio Workstation (DAW): Software designed primarily for recording, editing, and playback of digital audio.

Decay: The progressive reduction in amplitude of a sound or electrical signal over time.

Decibel (dB): The standard unit of measurement used to represent sound volume or sound level. In the digital audio world, it is often assumed that when referring to "dB", it actually refers to decibels relative to full scale (dBFS), where "0dBFS" represents the maximum possible digital level. This means that measurements in the digital audio realm are generally represented in negative values (-).

Distortion: The audio garble that is heard when an audio waveform has been altered. The distortion, which is undesirable in audiobook narration, usually occurs when the maximum output of an audio system is exceeded.

Dynamic Range: The ratio of the amplitude between the maximum and minimum sound levels in a recording. This ratio is usually expressed in decibels as the difference between the loudest possible undistorted level, and the level of the noise floor.

Edited Master: Raw audio (unprocessed) that has gone through the editing/quality control pass (QC pass) stage. This form of audio has not been processed a.k.a. mastered, but has been edited and corrected (QC pass).

Encoding: The process of converting your uncompressed audio files into a format more suitable for certain applications. In audiobook production, this often means converting WAV files to MP3.

Equalization (EQ): The process of boosting or attenuating frequency ranges for the purpose of enhancing sound.

Fader: Another term used for an audio level control, which today refers to a straight-line slide control, rather than a rotary control.

Frequency: The number of times an event repeats itself in a given period of time. Generally, the time period for audio frequencies is one second. Frequency is measured in cycles per second (Hz), and one Hz equals one cycle per second. One kHz (Kilohertz) is 1,000 cycles per second. The audio frequency range for human hearing is generally 20 Hz to 20,000 Hz. This range covers the fundamental pitch and most overtones of musical instruments.

Gain: The amount of amplification (voltage, current or power) of an audio signal, usually expressed in units of dB, i.e. the ratio of the output level to the input level.

Headroom: A term related to dynamic range expressed in decibels (dB), as the difference between the typical operating level, and the maximum operating level in an audio system. The maximum output level of a Digital Audible Workstation (DAW) is 0dB, though many DAWs have additional headroom built into the master fader which allows sound to be output between +3dBFS and +6dBFS. At Audible Studios, audiobook recordings are limited to a maximum peak of -3dB in order to leave headroom and avoid clipping (distortion caused by audio peaks exceeding 0dB). This limit allows for 3dB of headroom, leaving room for any surprise peaks that may occur when converting or exporting audiobooks to audible.com.

Interleaved Stereo: A stereo audio file that contains information for the left and right channels as one continuous block of data. If your files must be presented to listeners in stereo, encoding in this manner is required.

Joint Stereo: A type of stereo MP3 format which cycles through several different kinds of processes to determine the most optimal-sounding technique for a given frame of audio. This format is prone to errors and glitches. ACX does not accept Joint Stereo files.

Level: Also referred to as 'volume', level is the amount of signal strength or amplitude, especially the average amplitude.

Limiter: A type of compressor with a fast attack and release, and a fixed ratio of 20:1 or greater. The dynamic action effectively prevents the audio signal from rising above the output ceiling setting. **See "Brickwall limiting" also**.

MP3: A common audio format for consumer audio streaming or storage, as well as the standard of digital audio compression.

Mastering: The process of preparing and transferring an edited and mixed audio file to a data storage device; the source from which all copies will be produced (via methods such as pressing, duplication or replication). Typically, mastering involves dynamic processing, such as limiting, and tonal processing, such as equalization and filtering.

Mono: Single-channel sound playback, usually deriving from a single sound source.

Noise Floor: The level of the noise below the audio signal in decibels (dB). Generally considered to be the audible level of background noise in a recording, where no narration is taking place. **See "Room Tone" also**.

Noise Reduction (NR): A signal processing function used to reduce the amount of background noise, as well as, to lower the noise floor.

Normalize: The process of increasing all digital samples linearly, by the same amount, in order for the largest original sample to reach a given level, based on a peak or RMs value.

Peak: The maximum instantaneous level of a signal.

Phasing: A phenomenon that occurs when two similar audio signals engage one another in an interfering fashion, causing an undesirable 'sweeping' effect. This is most commonly heard when summing a stereo audio file into mono.

Production Master: The final, retail-ready audiobook. At this point, the audio has gone through the editing/quality control pass (QC pass) stage, and has been mastered (processed).

Q: An equalizer control that determines how wide or narrow the bandwidth of a selected frequency range will be.

Raw Audio: Unprocessed recorded audio, and the first state of your audio files before the editing/quality control pass (QC pass).

Root Mean Square (RMS): A conventional way to measure the effective average value of an audio signal as well as the perceived dynamic range values of that signal.

Room Tone: The background noise in a room. For audiobook purposes, room tone should be the resting sound in your studio, and as close to silence as possible.

Signal: A generic name used for audio recording purposes that refers to one of the many forms of sound in the audio chain.

Stereo Interleaved: See "Interleaved Stereo"

Threshold: The level at which a dynamics processor will activate, that is, begin to change gain.

VBR (Variable Bit Rate): An encoding option for audio files which tries to minimize file size by encoding to a sliding quality scale instead of a fixed bitrate. ACX does not accept VBR files.

WAV: The most common uncompressed audio format. You should record, edit, and master your audio as WAV files until you are ready to convert to MP3.

"Whatever the mind can conceive and believe, the mind can achieve."

- Napoleon Hill

Location, Location, Location!

Airbnb is one of the biggest things to happen to the travel industry in the past decade. On any one night, over two million people stay in homes advertised through Airbnb in 65,000 cities around the world. That's a lot of people spending a lot of time in other people's houses.

If you live in a desirable place, a big city, a room with a view, the chances are that someone would like to stay in your home for a few days. Airbnb connects those with a room/space to rent to those looking for a place to stay. If you live in a small town, near a racetrack, convention center, the sea or other venues where major sporting events are being held regularly, then you can rent your home out to people attending those events through Airbnb.

Airbnb allows guests to travel all around the world and to stay in accommodations that are less expensive than the local hotels. Airbnb breaks rentals into three categories: private room, shared room, or an entire home.
It's now easier than ever to make a profile and with their identification and safety process, you shouldn't have anyone in your home that you need to be overly cautious about.

Airbnb is great because you can earn money on a space you already own. It does require a little work up front to prep your place, list it, and potentially clean up after guests, but it is still passive income on a place you are not using much throughout the year.

Do you have a spare room, apartment, or a family house you use only on weekends or during the summer? Don't let your home or spare room sit around while you are not using it.
If you do not want to host your guests and see them in your private residence, having a private entrance is a MUST.

Thinking outside the box.

Here in the UK its very common for Hospitals to charge for parking. If you live near a hospital, why not rent out the driveway via Gumtree, a website or craigslist to people who need to go to the hospital for long periods but want to spend around 50% less than what the hospital charge for parking and are willing to walk for a few short minutes.

Here's how Air BnB works:

1. Sign up for a FREE Airbnb account
2. Fix up your spare bedroom (or entire house if you prefer and are maybe out of town, away on work, etc.)
3. List it on Airbnb, with as many enticing photos and interesting details as possible. Someone then comes to stay the duration agreed and pays you for the luxury.

Become a Superhost:

Airbnb launched their Superhost program in 2016 to reward their best hosts with a special VIP status badge. Beyond just a nice title, they allow hosts who achieve Airbnb Superhost status to reap benefits such as improved search placement, better booking conversions, and ultimately at the end of the day, more revenue.

How to Qualify for Airbnb Superhost Status

To become an Airbnb Superhost, you must do the following:

1. Host a minimum of 10 stays in a year
2. Respond to guests quickly and maintain a 90% response rate or higher.
3. Have at least 80% 5-star reviews
4. Honour confirmed reservations (hosts should rarely cancel)

Hosts who provide a predictable level of service will be rewarded with a status that could potentially lead to more bookings and increased revenue.

Airbnb Example: In 2014 my cousin Samuel bought a luxury apartment in Miami, and instead of renting to long-term renters at $1,650 a month, he decided to offer it up as an Airbnb rental. At $150 a night, he now earns on average of $3000-$4500 a month.

Airbnb Example 2: In my hometown (Birmingham) there is married couple I know that run their entire business model on what I am about to tell you. This strategy can be risky in unpredictable times, however, so if this sounds like something you would do, then proceed with caution.

This couple (the Millers) Purchase properties in desirable small towns just to rent out on Airbnb. They make 40% more revenue than renting out to long term renters and use that extra money to pay off their Mortgage quicker. A Mortgage that would usually take an average of 25 years to pay off, they are on track to have paid for 3 homes within 13 years. The Millers also rent out their homes as one-off cases. Renting it out on a case-by-case basis for days such as photo shoots, movie shoots, or even shoots for the adult industry.

To make this truly passive, you can use sites such as www.guesty.com and www.smartbnb.io to automate your messaging for people who ask the same type of questions all the time. Also, sites such as www.tidy.com will do all the cleaning up the next day. This is extremely effective for those that have a property in another city or country than they currently live in.

Why not download the app and have a read through the process?

Hot Tips:

1. It goes without saying that you need to have good pictures for your home. Take some time to do your research on the keywords your potential customers are looking for. Some hosts are earning six figures a year from implementing this simple idea.

    Airbnb Success Story:
    www.fastcompany.com/3043468/the-secrets-of-airbnb-superhosts

2. Reviews, reviews, reviews! The service you provide to your guests has to be to an excellent standard! You are entering into the hospitality business and you will be working with the public. This is your chance to sell yourself! How effective your listing profile is at turning potential guests into PAYING guests will be key.

3. Get a Yale touch screen deadlock for your front door. This locking system has a keycode input technology, that way you can simply change the passcode anytime you get a new person staying.

"Either you run the day, or the day runs you."

– Jim Rohn

Wrap It Up

You drive your car every day and it costs you money in tax, gas and insurance! What if there was a way you could make money with your car on an everyday basis? Now we are of course not talking about becoming an Uber or Lyft driver, we are talking about Car wrapped advertising!

A car wrap is a vibrant and colourful advert printed on a special quality vinyl covering, so it can be temporarily stuck onto your vehicle. Car-wrapping can be described in its simplest form as the process of entirely or partially covering a vehicle with full-colour images or call to action adverts.

If you commute to work, spend lots of time on the road or clock up a fair amount of miles per month, have a relatively new car (less than five years old), allowing a business to wrap your car with their advertisement in a short-term wrap campaign can earn you a monthly income while you drive around on the daily drive that you would be doing anyway. This can be quite lucrative, and the duration of the ad campaign can be anything from 30 to 365 days.

You may be asking yourself "What does a company get out of this type of ad strategy?"

They get lots of exposure. The wraps that they put on your car tend to be very colourful, eye-catching and attract lots of attention. It is also a form of advertising with a captive audience, meaning people who are stuck in traffic can't avoid seeing your wrapped car in front or alongside them. When an advertiser wants to promote in an area, they go to a car wrapped advertiser like www.wrapify.com/ for help. If a driver spends at least 25% of their commute in the advertiser's selected "campaign zone", they are notified that there is an opportunity to cash in on their commute.

If you remember the Red Bull cars driving around or have spotted a chiropractor or salon wrapped car, then chances are you remembered a car wrapped ad campaign.

The majority of people drive every day past an audience of thousands of people. This is marketing exposure that has significant value to brands. Advertisers provide a means for drivers to earn extra money for putting an ad on their car.

Before every installation appointment, the company installing will perform a thorough inspection to document the vehicle condition prior to the wrap application, and after the wrap has been removed.

I recommend speaking with your insurers before agreeing to have any advert applied. Most insurers have different policies and requirements when it comes to displaying adverts on your car.

Campaign lengths are selected by the Advertisers, and can range anywhere between 1-12 months. However, on average, most campaigns only last between 1-3 months long. The campaign durations are listed in the description of each offer (one month = 28 days). Remember, just because you received an offer, doesn't mean that you have to accept to put the ad onto your car. You could simply take a break for a few months and do it from time to time.

Some vehicles cannot be wrapped, these vary per site however typically the ones on the exclude list are motorcycles, commercial vehicles, transit vans, or any type of RV/motorhome.

Companies such as Car Quids, Carvertise, Wrapify and Ad Wraps are perfect for this.

Carvertise: Carvertise's earning potential is decent, you could make up to $1200 during a single ad campaign and can usually expect around $200 a month even as a newbie, just to use your car as ad space.

Car Quids: Car Quids matches drivers with advertisers, helping brands connect with millions of people every day. Drivers get paid each month, and for advertisers it is a unique form of marketing that creates buzz and sparks conversations in towns and cities up and down the UK.

Wrapify: Wrapify works similarly to Carvertise, but the main difference is in how you get paid. With Wrapify, you track your mileage and location using GPS. The more you drive, the more ads you qualify for, and the more money you take home, which can add up to around $200-$1000 a month for newbies.

How does Wrapify work?

1: Download the app from your phone's app store.
2: Drive 50 qualifying miles of your normal, everyday commute.
3: Review/Accept campaign offer.
4: Agree to Driver Terms and Conditions and submit a basic background check.
5: Take 4 pics of your car from the app. (front, back and each side)
6: Select an install shop location, date and time.
7: Drop your car off for your install appointment.
8: EARN WHILE YOU DRIVE!

Hot Tip:

These advertisements could help pay for your monthly car payments, and you may be able to pay off the car of your dreams a lot quicker than you think.

"A moment's insight is sometimes worth a life's experience."

— **OLIVER WENDELL HOLMES, SR**

Dividend Growth Formula

Gain passive income by building a portfolio of stocks that pay dividends, and receive quarterly or annual earnings from the companies that you invest in.

Before investing in any company, check whether earnings and revenues are growing and ensure it's not overly burdened with debt. All of these factors have an impact on payouts. The world's most famous investor, Warren Buffett, advocates looking for companies that enjoy an 'economic moat', by which he means firms with a very strong brand and competitive advantage in their marketplace.

When you invest remember that the growth of your portfolio depends on three interdependent factors:

1. The capital you invest.

2. How many net annual earnings are on your capital,
3. The number of years or period of your investment.

If you are starting with zero cash to invest, you should start saving as soon as possible, save as much as you can, to receive the highest return possible consistent with your risk philosophy.

Not all companies pay dividends. Either quarterly or annually however, companies such as Lloyds, BT, and Tesco provide good dividend returns. But don't get hung up on those, as there are many others out there.

Compounding

Dividends often provide an investor with the opportunity to take advantage of the power of compounding. Dividend compounding occurs when dividends are reinvested to purchase additional shares of stock, thereby resulting in higher profits.

To take advantage of the power of compounding, you need:

1. An initial investment,
2. Earnings (dividends, interest, etc.),
3. Reinvestment of earnings.
4. Time.

Tax

Dividends from companies in the UK generally don't have tax deducted at the source, but dividends from foreign companies might do – it all depends on their local rules. At present, in the UK the first £2,000 of dividends is tax-free, whatever rate of tax you pay, with the excess taxed at 7.5% for basic-rate taxpayers while higher and additional rate taxpayers pay 32.5% and 38.1% respectively. Any tax deducted at source under foreign rules may reduce the UK tax payable under UK rules. If you hold the shares in an ISA or a pension plan such as a SIPP then there's no tax on dividends, and you can reclaim some deductions at source.

Buying Shares

Generally, shares are bought through a stockbroker or a financial services firm. However, when a company first floats on the stock market, you can sometimes buy shares straight from the company. This is called an IPO (Initial Public Offering)

Apps to buy shares:

Trading 212: Trading 212 is a London based fintech company that democratises the financial markets with free, smart and easy to use apps, enabling anyone to trade equities, Forex, commodities and more. With over 14 million downloads, I recommend buying shares through this app because:

1. Trading 212 is authorised and regulated by the FCA (Financial Conduct Authority),

2. Your funds are kept in a segregated account and are protected by the FSCS for up to £85,000,
3. They also protect your data by implementing the industry's best practices,
4. They give you access to a dummy account to practice with £50,000 to spend.

Although not always the dividend strategy, I myself have bought stocks in Disney, Ripple, Shopify and Daimler AG (Mercedes) over the years and trust the use of this app and its security.

Plus500: Plus500 is a leading provider of Contracts for Difference (CFDs), delivering trading facilities on shares, forex, commodities, cryptocurrencies, ETFs, options and indices, alongside innovative trading technology. Plus500 also give you access to a Demo account to use and practice.

eToro: eToro takes great pride in its social trading features, enabling its clients to benefit from the collective wisdom of its vast network of traders. Their social newsfeed, CopyTrader™ system, and Popular Investor program utilise the full potential of a next-generation social trading platform. With numerous successful traders using their platform to share their strategies, eToro clients have everything they need to pursue their financial goals.

If you'd like to go through a stockbroker to look at your investment in more detail, two stockbrokers I recommend are:

1. Barclays – www.barclaysstockbrokers.co.uk
2. The Share Centre – www.share.com

Hot Tip:

Consider these things when looking at stockbrokers:

- **The cost of trading:** Every time you trade, you're paying the broker a fee so you may prefer something like a fixed fee or a percentage fee.

- **Account management fees:** In addition to the cost of making actual trades, some stockbrokers may also charge platform and account management fees.

- **International options:** Some of the best UK share broker companies, and online UK stockbrokers will offer the opportunity to do international trading or trading on stock exchanges outside of the UK.

"Formal education will make you a living; self-education will make you a fortune."

- Jim Rohn

Picasso Baby

If you fancy yourself the next Picasso, Michelangelo or simply love to sketch, paint or illustrate on your new iPad Pro, you can sell your artwork and prints (copies of your original) and make money passively online. Join the global online creative community of independent and emerging artists and start to receive passive income from your Artwork.

With just a few clicks, you can upload your images online, set your price, and instantly sell prints and copies of your art. Many websites will print your creations for you, insert your art into beautiful frames and then ship it to their customers.

Print-on-demand websites are an increasingly popular outlets for artists and designers to sell (or share) their passion online. What's especially appealing about print-on-demand is that once you've uploaded a high-quality image of your artwork, the site takes care of everything else – so you can get on with what you love, which is making more art. That high quality image will then be printed on anything from art prints to phone cases, t-shirts and pillows. Not every artist's work will sit happily on a phone skin or duvet cover – print-on-demand sites are more weighted towards graphic and illustrative styles but there's plenty of painters and fine artists selling their work there too.

One of the biggest challenges to selling your art online is getting traffic to your artwork. One great strategy in today's digital age is to team up with an existing platform. This allows you to take advantage of an existing audience and existing sales tools, without the need of developing them yourself. Showing your work in online art galleries or marketplaces allows you to expand your reach in the search for potential buyers. Buyers can narrow down their search using all kind of filters from art materials used to subject and price.

Commission fees are usually minimal, and you can still build a direct relationship with the people who buy your art and add them to your mailing list. Prints, and smaller original artworks can do well on marketplace sites so they can be a good steppingstone to selling your work at an online gallery once you've built up an audience.

There's no avoiding it these days, if you want to sell art online it's a lot easier if you employ the tools of social media to connect and engage with people who'll buy your work (or help you sell it). My tips for social media are simple. Find social media channels that work best for you. Instagram, Facebook, Snapchat and Pinterest are great tools to help boost sales, however you don't have to do them all! Choose the social media channels that you enjoy and work with them. If you have a good following base, you are already halfway there. You can also joint venture and use bloggers in your niche to advertise and get sales through the door. Remember social media is just a collective term for people communicating. People who, like us, happen to be using their smartphone, tablet or computer to connect with the world.

As I said, selling your art can be another great way of earning passive income; however, you should consider uploading your art (paintings, digital art, pattern designs) on multiple websites. This way you will be able to generate more income from the same artwork. Websites that you can sell your artwork on are available to you at a click of a button:

Best websites to upload your artwork are:

www.shutterstock.com
www.fotolia.com
www.istock.com
www.depositphoto.com
www.123rf.com

Best websites for print on demand are:

www.spoonflower.com
www.roostery.com

www.zazzle.com
www.redbubble.com

Vector patterns work well with these sites, and all high-quality artwork and photographs are accepted.

These images will also show up in Google images, so you can also be discovered there. And who knows? Someone might contact you for paid collaborations.

How to deal with copycats

Most of the websites listed above will protect your images by adding a branded watermark on to each image. If someone screenshots your artwork, it will have the watermark and branding still visible. If you've found someone that has lifted your artwork, start by contacting them yourself. Explain you are the original artist and they're using your work without your permission. Send a follow up email before considering legal action. Remember you do have rights, if you think you've been the victim of plagiarism, you are entitled to contact a copyright lawyer.

Special Bonus

Have you downloaded your FREE (£29.99 Value) bonuses yet? This includes a special PDF guide about niches. If not head over to:
www.businessmarketingfinance.com/readers

Hot Tips:

1. When writing a description try putting yourself in the mind of the buyer. They are not looking for an ocean painting with a lot of blue. They are looking for a striking piece of art for their hallway that will greet visitors with a warm blast of dazzling sunlight and evoke dreamy memories of the intoxicating salt air and the bright cobalt sea. How can you make them FEEL your artwork with words?

2. It's a good idea when converting your art into digital format to become competent in working with Illustrator and Photoshop, in order to get the best out of working with these sites and enable your artwork to be seen in its best light.

3. You can also use Google ads to drive traffic to your page on any of the platforms listed above. My advice is to make your ads as precise as possible. You want to keep your CPC (cost per click) down. Create a new ad for every single one of your new pieces of artwork, and include keywords or keyword phrases. Use those phrases in the title of your artwork or body of each ad. For each ad, target only that keyword and some simple variations.

"When you cease to dream, you cease to live."

-Malcolm Forbes

Music Made Easy

Earn royalties from your music or songwriting skills. This is one that is very close to my heart. After releasing many songs over a span of 16 years, I must say that this stream of passive income never gets old.

Just like stock photos you can license and earn a royalty off of your music when someone chooses to use or listen to it. Music is often licensed for YouTube videos, films, commercials, and more.

If you release a song that you have written the lyrics or produced the music for and own the publishing, you are owed royalties every time that song is played in a public setting. This includes radio, TV, movies, venues, restaurants and more. You are also owed a publishing royalty every time someone purchases or streams your music online through services such as: iTunes, Apple

Music, Tidal, Google Play, Spotify and Amazon (plus over 33 more).

Music publishing can generate a lot of passive income for songwriters, producers, composers, and lyricists.
This was probably my first ever passive income stream. Songs I produced over 12 years ago are still paying royalties each quarter.

If you have written or produced a song and haven't signed away the rights to someone else, then you are the publisher—which means that all royalties collected for that song should be paid to you.

Music ownership is managed via royalties. Having ownership of those rights means the holder earns money on the broadcast and streaming earnings of that music.

If you are not a songwriter, composer or producer, you can even buy someone else's share of a song via a writer's auction.

For example, if a songwriter dies, their heirs have the right to auction off a percentage of their songs during an estate sale. You bid on a song, and if it is accepted, you own a piece of it and receive a royalty cheque each month.

You can bid on owning music publishing on the site Royalty Exchange. Another good website for this is royaltyshare.com where you can buy the royalties from many music tracks, patents, and entertainment. You can find some excellent deals on these websites.

In 1985 Michael Jackson bought the publishing rights to the entire Beatles catalogue for $47.5 million giving him royalties on any compilation and play of any song in any public setting (Est 16 million per year).

PRS (Performing Right Society) in the UK and ASCAP (American Society of Composers, Authors, and Publishers) and BMI (Broadcast Music Inc.) in the USA are the agencies that will collect the broadcast royalties and get you paid what you are owed (typically on a quarterly basis)

Getting paid via streaming services such as Apple Music, Spotify and Tidal (plus over 30 others) has never been easier, and your music is usually distributed to these platforms via Distrokid, Tunecore, CD Baby or Ditto Music.

DISTROKID

Distrokid is a visionary company; they were the first company to offer unlimited distribution for a one-time annual fee of as low as £9.99. Uploading your music on this platform is straightforward.
They offer unlimited songs per year and their turnaround time for having your music posted to the streaming platforms is speedy! You keep 100% of your royalties as they charge no commission. They have a good add-on when you start the uploading of your tracks. Helping you with YouTube also.

One of these add-ons is a Leave Your Legacy add-on. This means that if you die or there is a lapse in payments to Distrokid, they will never remove your music from Spotify, apple music, etc.
Some of the add-ons are more expensive than the subscription, but you don't have to order them for every track.

DITTO

Ditto is another platform which charges no commission meaning you keep 100% of what is made. They also offer unlimited songs for one yearly price.
I've noticed there are a lot of hidden costs with Ditto, it is worth reading the small print with this service before choosing them. Their customer service could be a lot better, I must warn you.

TuneCore

Like Distrokid, TuneCore doesn't take any commission. You get to keep 100% of the royalties, and their analytic reports are on par with Distrokid as being some of the best around, allowing you to get an excellent insight into how well your music is doing.
Tunecore however charge a comparatively high yearly fee for each release, this is something that can add up over time.

CD BABY

CD baby has been around a long time (since 1998). There are no annual fees, meaning you just pay once for the service, and your music is up forever. CD Baby also offer physical distribution for your music to their very own marketplace. However, they do charge 9% commission for music streaming and 30% for YouTube distribution. Overall, I recommend Distrokid as they have great features, and the vision of the company is very innovative. If you would like to sign up to Distrokid here is a link for 9% off!

http://bit.ly/distrodiscount

If you are a music producer/composer, another great way to gain passive income is to set up a mini site on platforms such as Beatstars or Airbit.

BeatStars and Airbit are digital production marketplaces that allow music producers to license and sell beats, and also give away free beats.

A production duo, who go by the producer name Soundmasters, are making a killing on Airbit by following these 5 simple steps:

1. Make an account with Airbit,
2. Give away 2-3 free beats weekly, promoting them on social media and thier Youtube channel,
3. Use VidIQ to search for the best Tags to use on Youtube to get noticed.

4. If somebody wants to download any of the free beats, they first have to join a mailing list (sign up form),
5. Promote offers and new PAID beats to the mailing list.

Hot Tips:

1. Are you a Music producer or composer? See also the "Market Place Assets" Chapter and add your music to a marketplace.
2. Another good marketplace to look at is Musicore.uk. If approved, they handle all the marketing for you and with other producers on their platform you get the chance to be featured when those producers' followers come to this platform to order beats.

"An entrepreneur is someone who jumps off a cliff and builds a plane on the way down."

-Reid Hoffman

Subscription Success

The subscription-based business model is a model that charges customers a recurring fee (typically monthly or yearly) to access a product or service. With all the added value for customers, as well as increased lifetime customer support and ease of implementation for merchants; companies large and small are turning to subscriptions to increase revenue while providing unique and pleasing customer journeys.

Subscriptions offer a stable financial model rooted in recurring monthly revenue that can be built around almost every niche – from socks to baby products and pets. If there's an existing community around a product or category online, chances are you can build a subscription box around it.

If you can provide access to content or a repeatable service, it can help bring a consistent, scalable income your business can depend on. Usually, what separates good ideas from great ones is specificity. Being as detailed as possible when analysing your market fit, competitive analysis, and the customer profile (avatar) is the first steps in building a successful subscription business.

Membership Model
If you are an industry expert with techniques to teach, or knowledge to share, then this membership-based business model is for you.

With this model you can:

- Build an online community: by bringing together the most active and interested people in your niche.
- Monetize your content: by putting the top-level insights you wouldn't share on your YouTube channel or social media behind a paywall. You usually teach the "what" and the "why" on these channels and then the "how" only to those who sign up.

Musicians, DJ's producer example
For £12.99 a month, budding and experienced musicians/DJs/Producers can join their online community. Once subscribed, they get access to a wide range of educational videos that teach specific composition, DJ or production skills. You can cover hundreds of tips and techniques in one-off training videos, or short follow-along courses, breaking down your content into bite-sized strategies to tackle a wide range of problems. Users can interact as much, or as little as they want to. Unlike an

online course, they can learn as they go, and choose from a wide variety of topics. Or, they can just hang around for the discussions.

Subscription Box model
Subscription boxes deliver a group of products directly to your customer's front door.

With subscription boxes, customers receive new and exciting shipments from you each month, with new items inside. The box is delivered containing items that relate to that niche theme. This model works very well with socks, makeup products, alcoholic beverages and sweets/snacks.

Cooking Subscription Box example
For £19.99 customers subscribe to receive unique recipes, over the shoulder video of you cooking a meal, a featured guest podcast episode and a set of questions each month. However, to add a bit of mystery, you the box creator get to choose the theme for that month. This could be Italian, Caribbean, Greek etc.

All you can eat model
This subscription offers recurring billing functionality to provide your customers access to a service.
It allows you to create content and have your audience stream it anytime, anywhere, using your online platform. When subscribers purchase access to your streaming platform, they can watch any of the videos in the library of content, on multiple devices. And, every Monday for example, they're treated to something new.

All you can eat model example

The most recognizable examples of an access subscription are Amazon Prime and Netflix, where a customer is billed monthly or in Amazons case yearly in exchange for access to free next day shipping, music and TV etc.

Special Bonus

Have you downloaded your FREE (£29.99 Value) bonuses yet? This includes a special PDF guide about niches.
If not head over to:
www.businessmarketingfinance.com/readers

Also, you can recommend this book by sharing this link:
www.dmjpublishing.co.uk/30passiveincomeideas

Hot Tips:

1. These days people like to pay using a variety of methods. Make sure you are set up for Apple Pay., Google Pay as well as the usual PayPal and card providers.

2. Recurring and predictable revenue are key. Once you have customers onboard it is important that you keep them engaged and add value. It is important to remember that it is way more cost effective to retain customers, than it is to acquire new ones.

"Everyone has ideas. They may be too busy or lack the confidence or technical ability to carry them out. But I want to carry them out. It is a matter of getting up and doing it."

- **James Dyson**

Marketplace Assets

This one is for the photographers, video makers, web template designers, music producers, and graphic artists. Ever wondered where your favorite YouTube channel, websites, blogs, billboards and sometimes even magazines get their photos? Alternatively, how some of your favorite documentaries get cool cutaway video shots? These photos and videos are 7 times out of 10 bought from stock marketplace websites. Millions of design/film agencies and people around the world use stock marketplaces to purchase stock photos, video footage, music, motion graphic scenes for intros and promos, graphics and much more for their projects, online presence or promotions. Many marketplaces have a customer visit log well over 1 million a day.

The potential to get your product in front of customers and lift up your sales volume is simply staggering. Marketplaces are where the buyers are, in vast numbers!

If you enjoy photography, you can submit your photos to these marketplaces and receive a commission each time someone purchases one of them.

Deposit photos, Photodune, Shutterstock, Revostock & Videohive, are all great marketplaces to submit your assets.

Example: You are a photographer and have a collection of sunsets that you have captured whilst traveling over the years. Submit these sunsets to a stock photo marketplace, and every time someone who needs a sunset purchases your sunset stock image for their website, billboard, magazine, flyer or brochure you get paid. Stock photos are images that anyone can license for creative use. Rather than hire a photographer, designers can search a large database of photos and quickly find one that works for their project. Some of the most popular stock photos include people, travel destinations, animals, and food.

The same process applies for use of videos. If you own a drone and enjoy taking it out and capturing the night sky or your city skyline at dusk, then submit these videos to Shutterstock, Videohive (Envato) and Videoblocks.

Shutterstock is one of the best and most popular photo stock websites available today. Their history, reputation, quality of service and affordability make them a preference amongst many buyers across the world.

Videoblocks provides affordable subscriptions to high-quality stock video libraries. Like Shutterstock, video stock footage can be purchased separately or included via a subscription.

Envato Market is a collection of themed marketplaces, where creatives sell digital assets to help bring your ideas to life. Buy anything, from Photoshop actions and video footage to advanced WordPress themes and plugins. Envato is an excellent platform to add your content (photographs, music, 3D models, video footage, etc.) and once approved (guidelines apply for each category on their website) you will earn a dividend (between 50-90%) every time somebody purchases your work. You can now set the price of your assets which is a big plus.

Music tracks are often licensed for YouTube Videos, Podcasts, TV commercials, film soundtracks, public events and more, and these can be uploaded to Audiojungle. Audiojungle is a platform that offers streamlined, high-quality licensing for filmmakers and video creators. Members with a subscription have full and unlimited access to the site's entire musical catalog and/or SFX catalog.

As your sales grow you could hire people to specialise in specific areas like marketing or logistics. If your business gets better at marketing, sales will grow further. If you get more efficient at creating stock and coming up with productive strategies, costs will fall.

By now you are probably aware that good feedback/reviews are essential, but there are also requirements and guidelines to follow for each marketplace. Requirements about photo/music/video quality, product descriptions, length, formats and much more. You might feel like you do a great job with your product, but when you sell on marketplaces, they will be the judge of that, according to their own rules. Selling suspensions and bans are common, and good responsible content creators can get hit by them as well as the dishonest sellers.

Ways to stand out from the crowd

When it comes to stock photography, quality is definitely important, but you also need to focus on quantity. Why not play the numbers game? Shutterstock recommends setting a monthly goal for 50-100 images, so that you build momentum with your earnings. The more images you have in your portfolio, the more consistent your revenue stream will be. Also don't be afraid to create generic work, as long as it's useful to a certain niche or demographic. You also need to remember not to showcase any brands or individuals in your work, unless you have their permission to do so.

Things to remember

- Whether we are talking about design assets, video, photography or music, make sure you own the complete rights to your content, including any necessary releases. All music samples must be fully cleared.
- The content should have commercial appeal.

- Only submit your best work. The more professional, intentional, and organized your portfolio, the more attractive it is to a customer.

Hot Tips:

1. As always take some time to think about which genre or niche you would like to go into.
2. Make sure you read the guidelines and you are submitting your best work! You don't want to get that disappointed feeling of having your work rejected again and again.

3. Make sure you are using keywords in your titles and common words in your tags. Think like a shopper and follow success. Learn from items that have sold already, even if they are not the same as yours.

"Your time is limited, so don't waste it living someone else's life."

- Steve Jobs

Effective Network Marketing

Network marketing is a direct selling business model in which salespeople work independently, promoting products or services. Whoever recruited them encourages them to recruit and train more people (downline members). They then encourage the people they recruited to do the same, and so on.

You may be surprised to learn that the Network Marketing or MLM (multi-level marketing) industry is bigger than the Music Industry, Film Industry, and even the Video Gaming Industry. Predominantly dealing with sales, and a network/team to gain passive income. This one is for people looking for a part-time or flexible business with high rewards.

Are you describing a pyramid scheme?
Let me clear this up, some people will use the terms – Network Marketing, Ponzi Scheme and pyramid schemes

– interchangeably. However, their meanings are quite different.

Pyramid/Ponzi schemes

Fraudsters that set up and run pyramid, Ponzi schemes etc are **100% scams**. A scam is a scheme that tricks people out of their money
.
In a pyramid/ponzi scheme nothing is sold, even though those who run it say otherwise. Those in the scheme try to make money purely by recruiting new agents and getting them to do the same.

Network Marketing

A network marketing model is a legal business which sells products or services.

According to the Office of the Attorney General of South Dakota in the United States:
"Pyramid Schemes are, however, fraudulent schemes, disguised as an MLM strategy. The difference between a pyramid scheme and a lawful MLM program is that there is no real product that is sold in a pyramid scheme. Participants attempt to make money solely by recruiting new participants into the program."

Multi-Level Marketing vs Pyramid Schemes - South Dakota Consumer Protection
https://consumer.sd.gov/fastfacts/marketing.aspx

Direct selling means selling goods or services directly to consumers either at their homes or where they work. The

sale does not occur in a retail environment, i.e., it doesn't happen in a shop.
You cannot usually find direct-sales products in shops, supermarkets, or department stores. The only way to buy them is by contacting an agent directly.

Companies such as Herbal Life, Ann Summers and Avon are all examples of multi-level marketing companies. You can earn passive income through their compensation plans of network marketing by building a team. Getting a team together can be relatively easy if you follow the compound method of 2 by 2, in which you recruit just two people and then help them get their two people each, and so on and so on. Once you have a team, you can also earn commissions from the network bonuses in the compensation plan also.

Earn passive income through network marketing by building a team underneath you – also known as a downline. Once you have a large team, you can earn commissions off of their sales as well as your own, usually by just helping them to recruit.
In a network marketing business model, you earn commission on your own sales and also all sales of your downline team. The team under them contains those they recruited and trained, plus all the other teams under the ones those people recruited, and so on. Network marketing allows you to get paid for telling people about a company's products or services. Remember, talking is free!

Companies such as Nandos, Starbucks, and even Facebook do not advertise on TV, they get us (you and me) to use word of mouth to market their services and products. The only difference is they do not pay you to refer them or talk about them (word of mouth).

I know people who earn over £50,000 a month by sharing a 2-minute video and getting on a zoom call: no meetings, no pressuring friends and family, just a 2-minute video explaining the features and benefits of the fantastic product and a follow up zoom call.

Here are two quick ways in which you can grow your team:

1. Hold a webinar and/or event where you invite people to attend and you or your upline (the person who recruited you) takes them through your opportunity. After which you ask people to join this opportunity, once they enter or sign up, you ask these recruits (typically 2 out of 5 people will join) to bring five friends the following week. This will compound, and within four weeks you could have over 60-100 people within your downline earning commission off of their sales.

2. Another way I have discovered, which is relatively new to the network marketing industry is to use an automated webinar. In this model, you peak a person's interested who may be curious about making some extra money or the product itself by using a targeted ad (Facebook, Instagram, Google Ads). They then sign up to become a lead and watch your automated webinar presentation

any time of the day. You then have your unique sign up form for them after the presentation. So many of my associates have made great passive income through this new secret and haven't had to annoy their friends and family in the process!

Hot Tips:

1. Build globally as quickly as possible. You never know who can benefit from this opportunity while being on your team. Also, ensure you help and mentor those in your team, so that the process is being duplicated and you are leveraging your team's network too.

2. You can also use automated tutorial webinars. Your Upline can help you in teaching the best principles to your team and then automate the webinar and plug them in. Get them to duplicate the process and it's a win-win.

"The goal of retirement is to live off your assets, not on them."

— **Frank Eberhart**

Rethinking Real Estate

For decades this has been notoriously known as a very "solid" way to invest your money and efforts up front. Real Estate is currently on the list for top-ten creators of billionaires.

Property investing has paid off handsomely for many people, both in terms of income and capital gains. From my experience, it is essential that you go into it with your eyes wide open, acknowledging the potential advantages and disadvantages for yourself.
If you're looking to buy a property to rent and you're brand-new to the rental game,
think modest, stable and middle of the road.
Choose the right area, do your math, shop around for buy to let mortgages and you should do well.

I have attended high ticket weekend courses, paid online courses and had my own experiences in property

94

investing, and my latest rock-solid strategy has been as follows:

Purchase a BMV (Below market value) property for say less than £100,000 with a market value of £120,000+, re-decorate (you would be surprised how inexpensive this is) and then rent it out to generate a monthly income for yourself. The extra £20,000+ you can use as equity later in the year, to deposit and start the whole process over again using none of your own money. Repeat this as many times as you like. I have a good entrepreneur friend of mine who now has 16 properties (I will catch up with him one day). All were bought using this strategy.

Your income from rent should exceed the cost of the mortgage. This gives you positive cash flow. Great tip for this is, taking a decent sized four bedrooms+ home, add locks to the doors of each room and have an HMO (house with multiple occupancies) where the tenants share a communal bathroom and kitchen but only have their bedroom as private space. I have even seen this done with an en-suite two-bedroom flat in which the Living room was turned into a bigger bedroom (to make three bedrooms), and that tenant was charged a little more for the extra space.

Similarly, with the en-suite bathroom, you could charge extra for the luxury of not sharing a bathroom with other tenants. Helpful tip on this one, make sure you get monthly rent due from tenants as a collective that way the pressure will be on from you, the landlord, and other tenants if one person is late in paying their share of the rent.

This strategy works well with students if you are in a student accommodation prime location, near to a university for example. If not, this also works very well with working professionals near to city centres or commuting towns.

Rent to Rent is another approach. Rent to Rent is where you rent a property from a landlord, and the Landlord receives a fixed guaranteed rent. Another way of thinking about this is you are subletting from the owner. This is all legal and usually involves commercial or corporate tenancies, management agreements, leases, and guaranteed rent schemes.

Turnkey properties are fantastic. This is where you are offered properties in an area that gives you high returns of cash flow almost instantly. Many property investments can earn you a 3-8%. ROI. With Vision Properties (Based in Canada) your ROI is on average 26-32%.

If you don't want to deal with tenants and fixing faults and make this truly passive, you can outsource the running of the properties to a management company.

For some of you, this idea may resonate a lot more strongly than online passive income opportunities, and that's a good thing. Remember to diversify your passive income portfolio so that it doesn't run out. This is also a good way to make sure a recession or the change of market will not financially cripple you.

Hot Tips:
1. Property managers usually take anything from 5-10% of your rental income so be sure to factor that in your rental price. If you are living in the UK, I'd also advise joining a PIN (Property Investors Network) in your local area.

2. Commercial Real Estate Leasing: Having a business and needing property is no different to an individual needing property. If a company cannot afford to buy a building, then they will have to lease. Unlike individual/family homes, commercial buildings can command much higher rental fees and extended periods of a lease. You can even sublet a property. The only thing to keep in mind is that the risk is much higher if you struggle to find tenants to fill the commercial space/property.

Useful Real Estate Terms

1. Adjustable-rate mortgage
There are two types of conventional loans: the fixed-rate and the adjustable-rate mortgage. In an adjustable-rate mortgage, the interest rate can change over the course of the loan at five, seven, or ten-year intervals. For homeowners who plan to stay in their home for more than a few years, this is a risky loan, as rates can suddenly skyrocket depending on market conditions.
2. Amortization

This is the process of combining both interest and principal in payments, rather than simply paying off interest at the start. This allows you to build more equity in the home early on.

3. Appraisal

In order to get a loan from a bank to buy a home, you first need to get the home appraised so the bank can be sure they are lending the correct amount of money. The appraiser will determine the value of the home based on an examination of the property itself, as well as the sale price of comparable homes in the area.

4. Assessed value

This is how much a home is worth according to a public tax assessor. The assessor makes that determination in order to figure out how much city or state tax is owed.

5. Buyer's agent

This is the agent who represents the buyer in the home-buying process. On the other side is the listing agent, who represents the seller.

6. Cash reserves

The cash reserves consist of the money left over for the buyer after the down payment and the closing costs.

7. Closing

The closing refers to the meeting that takes place where the sale of the property is finalized. At the closing, buyers and sellers sign the final documents, and the buyer makes the down payment and pays closing costs.

8. Closing costs

In addition to the final price of a home, there are also closing costs, which will typically make up about two to five percent of the purchase price, not including the down payment. Examples of closings costs include loan processing costs, title insurance, and excise tax.

9. Comparative market analysis

Comparative market analysis (CMA) is a report on comparable homes in the area that is used to derive an accurate value for the home in question.

10. Contingencies

This term refers to conditions that have to be met in order for the purchase of a home to be finalized. For example, there may be contingencies that the loan must be approved, or the appraised value must be near the final sale price.

11. Dual agency

Dual agency is when one agent represents both sides, rather than having both a buyer's agent and a listing agent.

12. Equity

Equity is ownership. In homeownership, equity refers to how much of your home you actually own—meaning how much of the principal you've paid off. The more equity you have, the more financial flexibility you have, as you can refinance against whatever equity you've built. Put another way, equity is the difference between the fair market value of the home and the unpaid balance of the mortgage. If you have a £200,000 home, and you still owe £150,000 on it, you have £50,000 in equity.

13. Escrow

Escrow is an account that the lender sets up that receives monthly payments from the buyer.

14. Fixed-rate mortgage

There are two types of conventional loans: the fixed-rate and the adjustable-rate mortgage. In a fixed-rate mortgage, the interest rate stays the same throughout the life of the loan.

15. Home warranty

This warranty protects from future problems to things such as plumbing and heating, which can be extremely expensive to fix.

16. Inspection

Home inspections are required once a potential buyer makes an offer. Typically, they cost a few hundred dollars. The purpose is to check that the house's plumbing, foundation, appliances, and other features are up to code. Issues that may turn up during an inspection may factor into the negotiation on a final price. Failing to do an inspection may result in surprise costly repairs down the road for the home buyer.

17. Interest

This is the cost of borrowing money for a home. Interest is combined with principal to determine monthly mortgage payments. The longer a mortgage is, the more you will pay in interest when you have finally paid off the loan.

18. Listing

A listing is essentially a home that is for sale. The term gets its name from the fact that these homes are often "listed" on a website or in a publication.

19. Listing agent

This is the agent who represents the seller in the home-buying process. On the other side is the buyer's agent, who represents the buyer.

20. Mortgage broker

The broker is an individual or company that is responsible for taking care of all aspects of the deal between borrowers and lenders, whether that be originating the loan or placing it with a funding source such as a bank.

21. Offer

This is the initial price offered by a prospective buyer to the seller. A seller may accept the offer, reject it, or counter with a different offer.

22. Pre-approval letter

Before buying a home, a buyer can obtain a pre-approval letter from a bank, which provides an estimate on how much the bank will lend that person. This letter will help determine what the buyer can afford.

23. Principal

The principal is the amount of money borrowed to purchase a home. Paying off the principal allows a buyer to build equity in a home. Principal is combined with interest to determine the monthly mortgage payment.

24. Private mortgage insurance

Private mortgage insurance (PMI) is an insurance premium that the buyer pays to the lender in order to protect the lender from default on a mortgage. These insurance payments typically end once the buyer builds up 20% equity in a home.

25. Real estate agent

A real estate agent is a professional with a real estate license who works under a broker and assists both buyers and sellers in the home-buying process.

26. Real estate broker

A real estate broker is a real estate agent who has passed a state broker's exam and met a minimum number of transactions. These brokers are able to work on their own or hire their own agents.

27. Realtor

A Realtor is a real estate agent who specifically is a member of the National Association of Realtors. NAR has a code of standards and ethics that members must adhere to.

28. Refinancing

Refinancing is when you restructure your home loan, replacing your old loan with an entirely new loan that has different rates and payment structures. The main reason people refinance their home loans is to get a lower interest rate on their mortgage, and therefore lower not only the monthly payment but also the overall debt owed.

29. Title insurance

Title insurance is often required as part of the closing costs. It covers research into public records to ensure that the title is free and clear, and ready for sale. If you purchase a home and find out later that there are liens on the home, you'll be glad you had title insurance.

"Twenty years from now you will be more disappointed by the things that you didn't do than by the ones you did do. So, throw off the bowlines. Sail away from the safe harbour. Catch the trade winds in your sails. Explore. Dream. Discover."

- Mark Twain

Blogging Secrets

Blogging is a shortened form of weblog. For the online business owner, it's a great way to draw attention to your website, build credibility, and create value that will always be available to your audience. A blog can be a stand-alone site or part of your main website.

Blogging has been known to be even easier than writing an eBook. Yes, in the beginning, there will be no income. However, over time, you'll start to generate revenue from your blog. After 2-3 months or so, it can snowball. Potentially, it could earn you five or six figures per year, sometimes even more than this depending on your level of content.

Writing good content

1. Plan your blog content by choosing a topic, creating an outline, conducting research, and checking facts.

2. Craft a headline that is both informative and will capture readers' attentions.

3. Write your post, either through drafts in single sessions or writing paragraphs gradually.

4. Use images and infographics to enhance your post, improve its flow, add humor, and explain complex topics.

5. Edit your blog post. Make sure to avoid repetition, read your post aloud to check its flow, have someone else read it and provide feedback, keep sentences and paragraphs short.

Traffic

Once you have written your content you need to concentrate on getting the traffic coming in. Traffic is split into two sources:

Traffic you own

Organic traffic through SEO (Search Engine Optimsation), Social media channels and your own list that you have built up (email subscribers etc).

Traffic you don't own

Paid ads such as google and Facebook ads. Or partnerships such as paid for lists and influencers.

If you are having difficulty bringing in organic or paid traffic and you need help with SEO, then I recommend http://scaledm.co.uk/ (they do all online/offline marketing and advertising) and they can assist you with this.

Linking your blog with affiliate products

If you consistently use your blog and create a lot of value for many people, you can generate an extraordinary amount of passive income by sending your readers to quality associated products. Provide value to your readers, which drives traffic to your site, and then monetize it with affiliate links.

Affiliate payments can vary widely depending on the niche you choose, however you can make money from being an affiliate for all kinds of products: books on Amazon (any Amazon product actually), online tools and resources, music, online courses, physical products (health bars, food, etc.)
Many of my students get affiliate sales within 30 days of starting a blog. As you increasingly post to your blog, your site will start bringing in traffic whether you put in any additional time/effort or not.

To succeed with blogs and affiliate marketing, it is imperative that your blog/website focuses on a specific niche (e.g. juicing) and that you only affiliate for products in that area of interest (e.g. juicing machines, supplies, recipe eBooks, etc.). Your readers will trust your opinion and thus be convinced enough to be ready to buy, and they will click through to complete a purchase.
Remember, the more niche your website and topics are, the better.
If you created a generic blog that covered everything from music to technology and fitness, then you will not be a go-to source of information and thus have less traffic. Also, make sure that your niche has enough products to promote (20 or more). Consistency matters to your

audience. It matters less how often you post than how consistently. If you only have time to do one post a month, that post should come out on the same date and time each month.

An excellent way to stay consistent is to write several posts before you release the blog. That means if life gets in the way and you don't have time, you have a backlog of material you can consistently publish or schedule in advance.

Do you have a blog that you frequently add to? In just four easy steps you can increase your income:

1. Write good content that gets lots of traffic
2. Convert visitors into email subscribers
3. Send them content that builds trust
4. Sell products or services your audience wants

Blogs in the following sub-markets make the most money:
- Dating and relationship related blogs
- Money related blogs
- Diet and fitness related blogs

If you're launching a fitness related blog, it should have a sub-niche, i.e. Ketogenic diet, Atkins, detoxing, training for people over 50 years old or blogging about remedies for back pain and other bodily ailments. Pick the niche and stay on track.

Where do I go to find products to link to?

Take a moment to read the affiliate marketing chapter, however I recommend the following two to start with:

Click Bank

Unlike traditional affiliate platforms, Clickbank serves as a marketplace for both people who create products, and affiliates. Thus, both parties can make money together without complex paperwork or agreements.

Amazon Associates

With Amazon Associates you can earn up to 12% in advertising fees with the world's most trusted e-commerce leader.

ClickBank and Amazon affiliates are ideal for this type of passive income. Once you sign up you can promote other people's products, and find people who will promote your products, so you can potentially get a huge following for your site.

Check out gifts.com and cj.com (commission junction) as these are equally good sources to get a broad range of products to promote on your blog site for people to click on and purchase.

Get those subscribers in and start selling!

Hot Tips:

1. If you do not have a blog, there are lots of free blog-based sites to get you started, such as WordPress, BlogSpot, and blogger.

2. Another great tip is selling banner ad space to companies to advertise their products and services on your website. Many companies, are looking to purchase ad space on high traffic sites to then resell to their advertisers.

"We cannot let the future of our children be decided by their zip codes and family incomes."

— **Sharad Vivek Sagar**

Online Course Recipe

If you can write an eBook, then there is no reason why you cannot write or create an online course. This is another tried and tested method to leverage your time and effort by teaching something once and getting paid for it over and over again.

Even if you have not written an eBook yet, but you have a lot of knowledge or you are an authority in your field, you can create a course and sell your expertise online. If you are not an authority but know someone who is knowledgeable in their own field or industry, you can ask them to deliver a course for you, and you can split the profits.

With companies such as Udemy, Kajabi and Teachable, the market for online courses has never been better.

Udemy is an online platform that allows users to take online video courses on a wide array of subjects.

Many people know this, but what you may not know is that you can become a teacher on Udemy also. Here you can create your own video course and allow users to purchase it on their platform. This is a fantastic option if you are highly knowledgeable in a specific subject matter.

Become an Author, find a problem or niche course idea and make an online course. It may take four times longer than an eBook or blog post to create, but the rewards can be far more significant.

This passive income stream will open doors to making money by teaching people something new, specific and niche, e.g., How to adopt a child?

It is worth noting that some authors who have delivered three courses or more, make over $1,000,000 a year in residual income doing this.

As a former teacher, I enjoy teaching people new skills and improve the way they interact and think. The analytics section in Udemy will allow you to see which subjects have very few courses available, but are high in demand. This is crucial as many course topics can be quite saturated.

Here are some examples of topics that are currently under saturated but in high demand:

• Mental health
• Creating webinars & online content
• Public Relations

- Databases
- Domestic Violence
- Languages

Some online course platforms such as Lynda.com charge a monthly fee to their customers. For example, one could pay £29.99 a month to gain access to all the courses on their online platform. When royalties are generated using the monthly subscription method, the longer the duration a customer spends on your course, the higher your monthly share of the site's revenue.

Places to start for managing your own Udemy type site of monthly membership are: Teachable, Thinktific and my personal favorite, Kajabi.

Once you have a few courses under your belt, why not try creating several packages at different price points. Some people will want every course you offer, some will want 2-5 and some just a single course. You can include all courses at the highest price point and have a middle price point for the 2-5 courses and the lower price point for singular courses. This way you can receive the largest possible volume of orders based on the level of usage.

If you have a skill, know anything well (how to fix a laptop, how to make a quilt, how to do **anything)**, you can create a course for your passion. You can then reach out to bloggers in your niche, that publish similar content and joint venture with them by asking if they will offer it to their list (traffic) as a paid download on their website.

Once you have chosen a topic, and you know where you want the viewer to end up once they have finished the course, break it down into milestones. Those milestones will become modules for your course. Course duration can range from only needing to be 30mins-8hours (Avg just 2 hours).

I break the whole process down into 8 STEPS:

1. Choose a Profitable niche Idea,
2. Test Your Idea by consulting your network, friends and family,
3. Create a Course Outline (remember escape and arrive),
4. Create Your Course Content,
5. Get Your Course Online (to one of the platforms above),
6. Set a Price for Your Course (check others in your market),
7. Get Students for Your Course (using webinars, LinkedIn, social media and paid ads),
8. Launch Your Course!

You should also add 2-5 of the following bonuses:

- Checklists for completing the steps you recommend in your video lessons,
- Note sheets to supplement the lessons,
- Audio files for people listening while traveling,
- Glossary,

- Informative interviews with other experts in the industry,
- Next steps PDF help sheets.

Special Bonus

Have you downloaded your FREE (£29.99 Value) bonuses yet? This includes a special PDF guide about niches. If not head over to:

www.businessmarketingfinance.com/readers

Also, you can recommend this book by sharing this link:
www.dmjpublishing.co.uk/30passiveincomeideas

Hot Tips:

1. An excellent way to expand this income stream is to design a course and offer beginner, intermediate and advanced versions of the same course.

2. Highly recommended platforms are Udemy skills-based courses, and my personal favorite – Business Marketing Finance Hub, which will be launched this year in 2020.

3. You can even become an affiliate for Udemy and get 20% off the cost price if people purchase a course through your blog, website or simply your link shared on WhatsApp or Facebook! Business Marketing Finance Hub will also have an affiliate section — an excellent way to generate an income without owning or creating any courses.

"He who makes $25,000 annually through passive income is more enviable than he who earns $100,000 annually through a salary."

— **Mokokoma Mokhonoana**

Drop Shipping Blueprint

Let's say you've been thinking about opening your own online business. However, you are not sure what you should sell, don't have the storage for inventory or simply don't have any money to invest. All you need is a computer, an online store, basic understanding of online marketing, and you are ready to go. Drop shipping is where you, through your online store (e-commerce website) sell products straight from the manufacturer, that is then delivered directly from the manufacturer to the retailer or customer. As a result, you, the merchant, never see or handle the product.

Simply put, the customer visits your website, orders a product for the price that you set, and then the supplier ships it directly to the customer and you make a profit.

Drop shipping can be an excellent way to make passive income. You do not have to stock any products, incur overhead or storage costs and the supplier/manufacturer ships the item directly to your customers with your own branded invoices/return slips, etc. Might I add, this is extremely low risk as you do not have to pay your supplier anything until your customer pays you.

So how does it work, you ask? Create an online store through Shopify (14 day free trial), choose an online retail store that has the option for drop shipping (places like AliExpress, Wholesale Central, Sale Hoo, Kmart, Wayfarer, and Wholesale 2b, add their wholesale priced products to your site , you set the retail price, so you control the margins (usually 30-40% increase of the listed wholesale price), and then start to drive traffic to your new site through, YouTube, blogs, webinars, SEO etc.

To make this truly passive, from time to time some basic admin may be necessary to update product prices/descriptions or answer customer questions, however if you hire a virtual assistant in another time zone (i.e., USA, Philippines or China) for only a few hours a week to promote good quality products well, you can sit back and watch the sales come in.

Look for niche products (see more on the choosing your niche free bonus) or groups of products that are hard to buy locally or source online. Products that are in the £50-£150 range, seasonal, are cheap to ship and are pretty stable over time tend to work well.

Don't have the time or the expertise to create your website? Use eBay with the same formula or get a site on

Shopify and set it up in less than 20 minutes. Shopify is the best ecommerce platform out there today and has everything you need to enable you to sell online, and market your products through email and social media. Shopify also has great themes (some of them are free), tools and apps to have you set up and ready to sell within a few hours' even if you are a complete novice to building websites.

You can find suppliers on your own, however free Shopify Apps such as Oberlo give you access to 10 of thousands of products to sell from vetted suppliers and inventory updates. Orbelo will also import all the products, descriptions, images, and product variations for the products you have chosen from AliExpress at the click of a button.

Once you have chosen your niche, it is insanely quick and easy to get set up. Over the years I have sold Dog beds, baby clothes using AliExpress and, using the same model, I even sold Sex toys (UK supplier). The possibilities truly are endless once you've chosen your niche.

I recommend starting with any of these type of products:

- Gardening (shovels, rakes, mowers)
- Pets
- Outdoor equipment (outdoor furniture- tables, chairs, hammocks)
- Diving equipment
- Sports memorabilia

What if my customers are put off by the long delivery times from AliExpress?

I ran into this problem 5 years ago when I first started out in drop shipping baby clothing using the Orbelo method. Choose the e-packet shipping method when using a supplier. This is a little higher in shipping fees, however, products can be delivered within 7 days. As long as you are upfront with the delivery times and make this clear in your shipping policy and the information on your product page, before customers order, the 7 days waiting time isn't usually an issue. Your messaging should be clear to your potential buyers, however. I recommend saying something like this:

"Due to extremely high demand, Shipping for the _____ product will be delayed by _____ amount of days. Please allow _____ amount of days for your _____ (product) to arrive at your door."

It is important to note that not all suppliers will have long delivery times. I found suppliers for Pet accessories as well as Gardening equipment that are in the UK, and both offer next day delivery.

Hot Tips:

1. Your supplier needs to handle customer calls/returns and not just ship the product to the country your customer is in, but actually ship the product to their door.

2. A legitimate wholesaler will not show you wholesale prices unless you set up an account with them first. All accounts should also be FREE.

3. People buy because they trust a brand or a company. Make sure you ask for reviews from your consumers and have clear descriptions and titles! Remember, as my good friend Peter Thomson says, "Objections come from a lack of clarity."

4. Always remember to optimise your product descriptions and titles for higher ranking in search engines and use good imagery! If you choose Shopify, they will make it incredibly easy for you. The sales stats and report information are excellent too.

"It is only if the primary or only reason you do what you do is to make money that you will envy every random person who made or makes a lot of money (or money that exceeds what you made or make)."

— **Mokokoma Mokhonoana**

App Mastery

It makes a lot of sense to launch an app in today's digital age. The vast majority of the population utilize different mobile apps as part of their daily lifestyle.

Many of us own a smartphone or tablet with quite a few of our favorite apps downloaded onto it. Have you ever had a perfect idea for an app? If so, you could consider hiring a developer to create the app for you. Or maybe you want the satisfaction of doing it yourself. You could then sell it on the Apple & Android App stores to earn passive Income each time someone downloads it.

Examples of apps that are a good idea:

- A mindfulness app like Headspace is superb for being mindful and having balance
- A food ordering app like Just Eat (think sub-niche) that allows people to order and get their food delivered

- A transportation app like Uber helps people go from A to B – the other features are secondary
- A communication app like WhatsApp, where people can message, audio call or video call with friends and family all over the world through WIFI or data.

Hiring a developer

Info based apps are the easiest apps to create, while games and tutorial apps have proven to be more lucrative and more sought after. Many developers will be able to use frameworks such as ionic to write for both stores simultaneously, so you won't have to create an entirely separate version for IOS if developing on Android for example. Developers can be found everywhere, locally or online. If you are looking online, Upwork and Fiverr are good places to start. As always, read the reviews and use the filters that the website offers.

An idea of costs

The most influential factors which determine the final cost to build an app are:

- Complexity, and the number of app features,
- Back-end infrastructure and connected APIs,
- Complexity of UX/UI design,
- Inclusion of additional branded visual elements,
- Development approach (native, mobile web, hybrid, etc),
- Number of platforms to be developed on (iOS, Android, web, etc),
- Monetisation options.

Taking the average rate of £50 an hour, a basic application will cost around £5000 - £10,000. Medium complexity apps will cost between £35,000 and £70,000. The cost of really complex apps usually goes beyond £70,000.

Building your own

The 9 steps to make your own app are:

1. Choose your niche
2. Do some market research
3. Sketch out your app idea
4. Make your app's graphic design
5. Make the app with XCode and Swift or Buildbox
6. Build your apps landing page
7. Launch the app in the App Store
8. Market your app to reach the right people
9. Improve your app with user feedback

There are many app builders available today, some of these are Appery, Game Salad, and Mobile Roadie. However, if you are considering building a gaming app, then I recommend:

Buildbox

Buildbox gives you the power to create 2d & 3d mobile games without using any code.
Using this platform, you can create amazing games regardless of your technical skills! They make the process really easy with tutorials and help you to publish to iOS & Android straight from the software itself. They offer easy

monetization, a game wizard, brainboxes, included smart assets and have a FREE plan available for you to get started and play around.

Monetization

Once you have uploaded your app to an app store, you can decide if it will be downloaded either paid or free. When creating a free app for your users, it is recommended to have both in-app purchases and click-through ads, where you can further increase your monthly income. By using sites such as Google AdMob, you can manage your advertising and send your consumers ads relevant to your industry. Thus, you can earn money every time a user clicks on that ad (even if by mistake).

In-app purchasing is big right now, and almost all games feature the ability to upgrade weapons, buy more game currency or merely have a new outfit for your character. The best example for this is Fortnite. It's a free game that generates 1.5 Million a day through in-app purchases, making this a perfect stream of passive income. As people have become used to getting these add-ons, I'd recommend adding in-app purchasing to pop up on the screen around national holidays and payday weekends for the impulse buyers out there to purchase extra content. Once they have completed one purchase, chances are they will buy again. Why not offer them another upsell deal each week that's centered around something they need and a little extra in price?

You can even reskin existing apps or create similar apps that solve a slightly different pain or re-targeted at a somewhat different niche audience or designed marginally better.

Special Bonus

Have you downloaded your FREE (£29.99 Value) bonuses yet? This includes a special PDF guide about niches. If not head over to:
www.businessmarketingfinance.com/readers

Also, you can recommend this book by sharing this link:
www.dmjpublishing.co.uk/30passiveincomeideas

Hot Tips:

1. If you already have a social media audience, then you can market your app through your website and also the people you engage with all the time. For those who want to make some money, you can also set a comp-plan and invite people to become affiliates for your app.

2. Use Facebook ads and target groups and blogs in your niche who may be interested in your app.

"Never depend on a single income. Make Investments and create a second source."

-Warren Buffet"

Crushing YouTube

YouTube was founded by former PayPal employees Chad Hurley, Steve Chen, and Jawed Karim. The idea was born at a dinner party in San Francisco about a year before its official launch in 2005. Today, the majority of people in the world would rather watch ten videos back to back than to read 1-2 pages of a book. Since its launch, YouTube has come a long way. Many advertisers are seeing the potential in reaching the incredible 1 Billion+ viewers per day (huge audience), and they all want in.

Anyone with a Gmail account can start to upload videos using this platform. If you have been told that you have a bubbly personality or you enjoy reviewing products, or giving your opinion on a subject, then this is a great one for you.

Equipment
Although it is important to make sure the video is as good as possible (high-quality), you will be surprised to know

that your smartphone may just be all you need in order to start. Many phones these days record in 4K and if you get a Bluetooth lapel mic you'll be on your way.

There are many topics you could create videos on and gain incredible amounts by monetizing your videos.

Monetization

YouTube monetization is fairly straightforward. Through Google ads, companies can create advertisements that get placed at the beginning, part way and/or end of your videos. These are called pre-roll ads. Each time a viewer watches an ad all the way through, you get paid.

Monetization Set up (getting money through advertising).

1. For YouTube channel creation, go to the "my channel settings" and enable your channel for monetisation.
2. Connect your YouTube channel to an AdSense account to earn more money and get paid for your monetised videos.
3. Take a minute to get to know the kinds of videos you can monetise and the different ad formats using YouTube tips/help sections.
4. YouTube updated their criteria in 2018. You now need a minimum of 4000 watched hours and a minimum of 1000 subscribers within 12 months to be able to turn on monetization for your channel.

The "time vs. reward" ratio is excellent, e.g., once set up, creating a video for YouTube on a topic takes 10-15 minutes, whereas writing the equivalent for a blog or book, could take an hour plus.

Comedy/Entertainment is YouTube's most popular category.

There are so many topics to choose from:

• Tutorials
• Become a Personality
• Film or music Reviews
• Food
• Web TV Series
• Feature your child or pet playing with a toy
• And the list goes on

Google (Who own the YouTube platform), massively favour YouTube in their search results, often putting videos for the search term at or near the top of search results without having ascertained the quality of the video. Google judges its relevance based on its title, description, and tags.

It is important to mention that the best way to rack up your views is to turn your video into a weekly series. That way, even if a viewer joins you on the step 6 video for example, they will have to go back and watch steps 1-5 to be brought up to speed.

Websites such as Social Blade can tell you how much money some of the highest earners are earning in each category on YouTube, just from monetizing.

One of YouTube's top earners, Ryan Kaji, an 8 years old, made $26million in 2019 and $22 million in 2018 by monetizing his videos. His videos are simply of him making toy review videos on anything from Pokémon to Dragonball Z.

Subscribers
24 Million

2019 Passive Earnings
$26 million

Total Views
12.3 billion

Speaking of making video content around your passion, Evan Fong age 27, known online as VanossGaming, is a Canadian internet personality, video game commentator, and music producer. He posts montage-style videos on YouTube of him and other creators playing some of the latest video games.

Subscribers
482,000

2019 Passive Earnings
$11.5 million

Total Views
12.3 billion

Go to related channels list on some heavy hitters' profiles and write them down. Go in the comments and see what people are saying so you know the audience and what they need. The above examples didn't happen overnight, however, as long as you keep uploading good content, you can earn as much as you want!

Hot Tips:

1. Pick a technical topic to record videos on, i.e., problem-solving topics. So, when they watch your video and a relevant ad pops up, they are more likely to click that product or service, and you get paid.

2. Make sure that the link to your website is in the first line of your video descriptions, so that you can funnel your YouTube traffic to your site.

3. If you use any equipment to make your videos, such as Camera, Laptop, Microphone, editing software, etc. then make sure you also add the affiliate links to these products with Amazon affiliates and earn even more income.

"A hard lesson I learned recently; when you are not making an income, you must surrender to some outcomes."

— **Robert Wesley Miller**

Web Hosting From Anywhere

At one of my companies, Scale DM (Digital Marketing company), I resell hosting to some of my clients who either do not have hosting when they come to us for a website, or they are unhappy with the extra bundled fees that their current provider is charging them. Reseller services are when you are essentially a middleman between service providers and clients. Other examples of this could be reselling Pay Point terminals, utility services and many more.

Reseller hosting is a form of web hosting where the account owner has the ability to use his or her allotted hard drive space and bandwidth to host websites on behalf of third parties. The reseller purchases the host's services wholesale and then sells them to customers, possibly for a profit. This form of hosting is often the easiest way to begin a hosting business. By using one control panel, you can manage multiple clients who will also have access to their own (limited) control panel to make changes and updates to their service. Many clients may not have knowledge or a background in this area and will be completely dependent on you for setup and changes to their service. This allows you, the reseller, to charge a bit more for this hands-on service. Shared hosting is usually located on a server which you will share with other hosting companies and individuals.

You can resell web hosting by purchasing a reseller account with a web hosting company that offers this program, such as the number 1 in the market right now, Blue Host. You do not have to own a data centre or have any cloud servers. You only sell the web hosting services as a third-party. The best thing about reselling hosting is that you do not need to deal with technical problems at all. All you have to do is to sell the space and bandwidth as your own branded web hosting company.

Becoming a web hosting reseller could be compared to running a bed and breakfast. By making your home available to clients, you're able to generate revenue without having to hire contractors to build a brand-new hotel. The best reseller web hosting opportunities enable you to start a new business without a prohibitive investment or decades of experience.
To really succeed, however, you'll want to spend the time learning about the tools and technologies that will help you on your journey. You also need to develop a business plan that outlines the steps to lasting profitability.

Before becoming a web hosting reseller, you need to make sure that your hosting provider is fast, reliable and has an excellent customer support system. They will answer your clients' tickets and deal with any complaints that they may have.

Make sure that the company you choose have the following:

- Top reviews and outstanding brand reputation
- They maintain quality service and feedback from their clients is at a high standard with 24/7 support.
- Icon_outlined_speed_caching
- Solutions for a wide range of users

Excellent and popular websites for this are:

- Blue Hosting
- Go Daddy
- HostGator
- TSO Hosting

You will need

- A powerful, reliable computer for running your web hosting business (Having a laptop will allow you to work from anywhere).
- High speed internet. Get the best you can afford.
- A phone line dedicated to the business
- A tax license, and an incorporation entity – I recommend becoming a Limited company.
- A Business bank account with your company name.

- A merchant account and gateway software for taking credit cards such as stripe or GoCardless.
- I also suggest a private work area in your home or office with a comfortable chair.
- Get a website built by a web design agency such as Scale DM. Team up with a developer or make your own using WordPress.

Additional ways to gain passive income through webhosting.

Become a Bluehost affiliate
Back in 2013, one of the first ways I started out was to simply promote Bluehost on my website with custom banners and links. For every visitor who clicked through these links and signed up, I received $65.

To set up with Bluehost.com, simply go to their website, click on the signup button and create an account. Once you set this up, you can click on the banner links section, and here you will find the links that you can use to promote the blue host program, and you can send this to your social media, targeting those who want to make their website or embed it on your site or blog sidebar.

Hot Tip:

Help your clients, and they will help you in return. A real positive review about your company can boost your credibility and reputation.

"My rich dad taught me to focus on passive income and spend my time acquiring the assets that provide passive or long-term residual income...passive income from capital gains, dividends, residual income from business, rental income from real estate, and royalties."

- Robert Kiyosaki

Online System Franchising

Online System Franchising is a license granted by an individual or business to another business in order to make and sell goods or services.
An online system describes the rationale of how a business creates, delivers, and captures value (economic, social, or other forms of value). The process of this system's construction is part of its business strategy and the design of organizational structures. The essence of an online system is that it defines the manner by which the business enterprises deliver value to their customers, entice customers to pay for value, and convert those payments to profit.

Ultimately, the online system is a simplified representation of its business logic. It describes what a company offers its customers, how it reaches them and relates to them, through which online resources, activities and partners it achieves this and finally, how it earns money.

This passive income stream is great if you have figured out a systematic way of running an online business. This can be e-commerce using Shopify, Magento or another online system.

Example

Let's say using Kajabi you create a successful online course for Teaching students how to take the PTTLs exam (entrance exam) successfully. You have a system that outlines the approach, course break down, learning materials/assets as well as the logo and other branding elements — something you can repeat again and again regardless of the industry.

In doing so, you have created a system that can be packaged to include: course creation, design, SEO, marketing, the handouts/assets, the website, the payments system, the social media strategy, etc.

You can then start charging a monthly fee for implementing this system into someone else's business, which is usually a percentage of their gross turnover to other people looking to profit from their relevant knowledge.

Franchising this way doesn't have to be a long-term partnership make sure you provide comprehensive training and Undertake ongoing research & development.

How?

Once you have the framework to **a system**, get in touch with experts in other fields, e.g., accountancy entrance exams, medical entrance exams, law entrance exams, etc.

You sell them the system for a monthly stake. You can even get a virtual assistant in the United States or the Philippines, for example, to set it all up for them, for an extra one-off fee.

This is more than an online course since you work side-by-side with them to make sure they launch the system properly and can maintain it. Then you take a percentage of profits. However, once the system is created, it can allow you to duplicate again and again for many industries.

"To obtain financial freedom, one must be either a business owner, an investor or both, generating passive income, particularly on a monthly basis."

- Robert Kiyosaki

Silent Partner Tactics

You can become a silent partner by entering into a limited partnership agreement with another person. The other person is the general partner, and they will be responsible for managing the business on a day-to-day basis. A silent partner is basically an individual whose involvement in a partnership is limited to providing capital to the business. A silent partner is seldom involved in the partnership's daily operations and does not generally participate in management meetings.

If you do your research on the business as well as your potential partner well enough, this can be an excellent source of passive income. The critical thing to remember here is that you only invest in a company that you can gain monthly cash flow from, on a consistent and ongoing basis. If you have a high net worth and money to invest in an enterprise, but you don't want to be involved in the decision-making or spend the time/effort helping the business grow, and still see a significant return on your investment, then this one is for you.

As with other partnership agreements, a silent partnership generally calls for a formal agreement in writing. Prior to the formation of a silent partnership, the business must be registered either as a general partnership or a limited liability partnership.

A partnership agreement designates which parties are general partners or silent partners. This serves as an outline to which functions, both financial and operational, the general partner will perform as well as the financial obligations that are assumed by the silent partner. Additionally, it includes the earnings percentage due to each partner in regard to business profits.

Silent partners are liable for any losses in the business up to their invested capital amount, as well as any liability they have assumed as part of the creation of the business. Participating as a silent partner is a suitable form of investment for those who want to have a stake in a growing business without exposing themselves to unlimited liability.

Contracts should include terms for buying out the ownership stake held by a silent partner, or otherwise dissolving the partnership. An entrepreneur starting a business might welcome the capital provided by a silent partner when getting his business off the ground. However, if the business becomes successful, it may become preferable to buy out the silent partner rather than share profits long-term.

If you know anybody locally that has a successful businesses and has years of experience, but they just need a little extra cash in order to expand or add an additional product line for example, then you could be the person to fund this, and you can both split the profits even though you are not managing the day to day operations or running the business.

A great classic example of this: Say you have a friend/associate who owns a hair salon that is doing well and now wants to expand with a second shop, in a reliable location with lots of footfall. This friend also wants to create their own product line of shampoos and conditioners.
If they have the expertise and experience and are only missing the capital to inject into the business, why not be the one to provide this investment and become their silent partner?
They will still be in charge of the day to day running of the business, but you will have a share of the profits, depending upon the agreement you reach together.

Angel Investing
An angel investor is an individual who provides capital for a business start-up, usually in exchange for convertible debt or ownership equity. Angel investors give support to start-ups at the initial moments, when most investors are not prepared to back them.

If you do not have a business locally or someone that you know of that you could partner up with, or simply just like the idea of investing in a start-up, then there are websites such as www.angel.co where they have vetted start-up businesses that you can search, invest in and share the profits!

AngelList

With over 5000 companies invested in, AngelList is basically like Match.com for start-ups, helping them get connected to both investors and employees.
AngelList is a platform for startups to receive funding online. It was founded in Jan 2010 by Babak Nivi and Naval Ravikant, who also wrote "Venture Hacks".

Angel Investing Networks

An Angel investor network is a collective of Angel investors who club together to network, share introductions and often syndicate their capital into a larger pot to make larger investments. Think of it as an alternative to a venture capital (VC) fund. It is less corporate and more diverse, more personal.

You can become an angel investor to one of over 95,000 companies, where you give money to start-ups in need of traction in exchange for equity. With AngelList, you can earn passively, diversify your portfolio, and support a start-up in lack of investment. Although there is no concrete rule dictating how much equity an angel investor will take in exchange for financial support, the general expectation is between 20% and 40%.

Shows such as Shark Tank and Dragons Den are good examples of angel investing.

An excellent place to buy a share of a high-quality business entity is www.businessesforsale.com or www.latonas.com (use the filters on these websites to get the business that is right for you).

Something you may also be interested in...

Ever thought of buying a site or app that already has a significant traffic/user base? What you are doing here is purchasing a dividend and buying the revenue from the person who hosts the site. Websites such as www.flippa.com and www.exchangemarketplace.com (Shopify exchange) are excellent sources for this. Flippa and Shopify exchange are marketplaces for budding entrepreneurs to discover new business ventures to invest in. Flippa is the world's number one source for buying and selling web businesses, domain names and mobile apps.

On both platforms, you can buy websites that earn you passive income from either advertising or drop shipping. Be wary of sites that don't list the NET Profit. You want to be as little involved in the website as possible.

Make sure you are getting virtual assistance, the customer list, and not just the domain name or website shell.

There are a few things to take into consideration here.

1. Does the site on offer generate the right amount of income for the original investment you will be making?

2. Can you add value to this business's website, for example, additional products or a marketing strategy to further increase your residual income?

3. Is there any maintenance required for this web-based business, or could a virtual assistant handle it once a month?

Also, always make sure that you know that you are purchasing a full package here. i.e., Domain name, Website, Customer list (important), and inventory.

Hot Tips for the silent partner

1. Make sure that the agreement is clear and highlights exactly the roles/responsibilities, decision making, capital contributions, dispute resolutions and liabilities of each member involved.

2. Do your homework (analysis, interviews, calls, references) and then diversify, diversify, diversify. Never put more than 5% of your wealth into this asset. You should diversify your investments and build a portfolio of 10 companies at least. Then,

make follow-on investments in the top performers of your portfolio.

Hot Tips for buying an existing online business:

1. Traffic stats are crucial. Make sure you know all the details of the website business you are purchasing, i.e. how many people are visiting/purchasing, per month.

2. It's worth noting that upon investigation some domain names have sold for £10,000 due to them being in demand.

"Residual income is passive income that comes in every month whether you show up or not. It is when you no longer get paid for your personal efforts alone, but you get paid on the efforts of hundreds or even thousands of others and on the efforts of your money! It's one of the keys to financial freedom and time freedom."

- Steve Fisher

Merch By Design

If you have any design talent, this can be a very cool idea. And if you don't know where to start in designing, try using Canva.

Canva, mentioned in the previous chapters, is a good place to start. Canva has many royalty free templates for you to choose from and has elements, fonts and even photos available for you to use. Go to www.canva.com and access the free version of their site, although I recommend paying for the pro version at $12.99 pcm.

Sites like CafePress make it simple to submit your creative designs on their online platform. This means that you can pump out a ton of designs in a few afternoons, add them on various merchandise such as water bottles, hats, aprons, stationary (so much more) and then leave them up there waiting for people to buy.

CafePress is a company that works with designers to give the world millions of designs on hundreds of different products. Their mission is to create human connection by inspiring people to express themselves.

There are no upfront fees for starting your own store, and you do not have to concern yourself with inventory or anything like that. Just create the designs, set up your store and pick the products you want your designs on. CafePress currently has over 250 different products for sale.

CafePress Promise

CafePress promises that you'll be completely satisfied, or they will 100% make it right. They produce every item on-demand and If you're not pleased with the product for any reason, you can return or exchange it for free within 30 days - even if it's personalised!

The key to making money with this idea is to design stuff for niches you know, e.g., computer geeks, people of faith, or even Star Wars fans!

I sat down with one web/graphic designer whom I've known for about a decade, and he uses this idea well. He has pumped out dozens of designs that involve HTML and CSS jokes such as "You are the CSS to my HTML" and is killing it on café express. Relative to the amount of time invested in the initial design work he is still getting a very healthy return, two and three years after putting them on this site.

Think about the number of niches that attract super passionate followers.

CafePress takes care of all the customer relations on their site including:
• Overall shopping experience for your customers, hosted on their servers.
• Secure checkout and credit card payment processing.
• They ship products worldwide.
• Phone, email & chatting customer support.
• Promotional tools to drive traffic to your shop.
• CafePress-sponsored promotions & sales.

Here is another example of a niche purchase, a friend of mine once bought 12 Camping themed mugs from CafeExpress because he and his recent in-laws were going camping that summer and he wanted to impress them with a cup that said "Camp we all get along?". This went down a treat and it lightened the mood for the weekend.

Hot Tips:

1. A big secret is to go for volume, e.g., 100 designs/photos on ten different products = 1000 products for sale. Try to also send your 10-100 designs to a Virtual Assistant, along with the categories/products you want them to upload, because this is going to take hours of tedious uploading and configurating.

2. You have to be careful when setting your mark-up, and make sure to always consider the base price. If CafePress is charging £15 base price to make a hat, and you then add another £10 or £15 of your own on there, your hat may not sell.

3. You can earn shop performance bonuses if you sell over £100 in products. This bonus ranges from an extra 10 to 30 percent.
4. If you allow your products to be included in the CafePress marketplace, you can earn 10% total on all sales from that marketplace.

5. While operating in the United States, Café express is now available in many other countries, including Europe, United Kingdom, Singapore, Canada and Israel.

"You become financially free when your passive income exceeds your expenses."

- T. Harv Eker

Affiliate Marketing System

The opportunity to make solid passive income doing affiliate marketing has never been better. Affiliate marketing is simply partnering with a company (becoming their affiliate) to receive a commission on a product that you promote through your content. This isn't always easy. Affiliate marketing becomes a passive income when you work hard for it. However, if you currently have a strong list or a lot of traffic going to your website or YouTube channel, and are not sure what to do with it, this one is for you.

If you are just starting out, don't worry, the first thing to do here is spend some time thinking about what niche you want to make your content for. You need to establish yourself as the "go-to" person on the topic of your choosing. I have a passion for Music and Marketing, so all of my affiliate products revolve around those topics. Any time I make content around these two topics, I have links to equipment or software that my audience can use.

When thinking about products to promote, it makes sense to sell things within your industry. For example, if you have a website or regularly speak about gardening, it would make sense to promote gardening products.
You can make videos or write articles on "The top 10 plants to grow in your garden for the X year" or "How to get more flowers and less weeds using X product". Simply swap out X result using X platform. Whatever niche you decide on, you need to find a niche you like, as you will be creating content around this and sending those who love and engage with you to your affiliate links. You need to make as much content as possible, having 10 articles on your website or 10 videos on YouTube about photography like my good friend Chris Winter, is a safe bet. A great way to make sure you are at the end of the buying cycle for someone interested in a product in your niche, is to do tutorials and reviews on products. You have probably seen a few videos while looking for a product yourself. These same videos usually have links in the description for you to purchase the product mentioned or read more about it. 9/10 these are affiliate links!

One of the easiest platforms to go on is Amazon Affiliates. Amazon continues to grow year by year and has an enormous number of customers looking to purchase products online.

Amazon currently makes up 49% of all online revenue. Which is HUGE!

Some people may not know this, but Shopify has a great affiliate program to get into as well. With Shopify affiliates, you earn an average of $58 for each user who signs up for a paid plan using your unique referral link, and $2000 for each Shopify Plus referral. Chris, whom I mentioned earlier, made over $40k in his first year only by promoting Shopify.

Get products that are relatively high on sale price, as commission payouts on Amazon are usually around 10%.

You earn a commission when you send someone to Amazon using your link. If they then buy anything else on Amazon within 24 hours, you get that commission also, whether they end up buying the product you promoted or not. For example, if you promoted a book and the person you sent to Amazon also ended up buying a hair dryer because they liked the look of a featured ad - you will get the commission for both.

The process of finding and selling products using Amazon's service can be started quickly with little to no start-up cost.

Making money with affiliate marketing programs is simple, and you only have to take your affiliate link and put it on your website, blog, YouTube channel or social media accounts for people to click on, which is how your pay is tracked.

Amazon has made it incredibly easy for customers to find the best-selling products site-wide and across all their niches.

Once you have researched a product, you then go to Amazon associates, sign up, and select the product you want to sell via your website, blog or social media platform (Facebook, Instagram, etc.) and then use the affiliate code. Now, when people purchase from this link, you earn a commission.

Let's say your blog or website is about car wrapping Mercedes cars. You regularly post content that engages with your audience, and they now trust your opinion. You could promote car accessories such as air fresheners, car mats, etc. on your site through Amazon associates.

Great affiliate marketing programs are all the range these days, and you can sell many items from major online stores and brands. From experience I recommend the following:

- Amazon
- Click Funnels
- Teachable
- Click Bank
- Bluehost
- Shopify

There are hundreds of affiliate programs out there, and most retailers have their sites listed in a "hub" for affiliate programs, where you can find the majority of their products.

I like the teachable model most as you receive 30% recurring commissions each month for whoever signs up through your link. That means if someone signs up for their regular plan, currently at $99, you will receive $29.70 ever single month until they cancel. The cookie lasts for 90 days, so whoever signs up within this time, you will receive the monthly commissions until they cancel their subscription.

Click bank is a great online affiliate marketplace where you can search for products that you can potentially promote on YouTube, Blogs, Websites, etc. Just make sure you ALWAYS promote a product you believe in. Affiliates can earn between 50-75% commission on anything from Diet pills to Software.

Once you have signed up, you are ready in just 3 easy steps:

1. Pick a category.
2. Find a Product.
3. Click on promote to get your affiliate hoplink.

Once you have the link, you can promote this using Facebook, Instagram, google ads and do a YouTube review on it. Alternatively, you can use your own list and website. When people buy using your link - you've guessed it - you earn 50-75% commission on that sale.

As your hoplink can be quite long, I'd also advise shortening it via a website like bit.ly to then post a shortened version for people to click.

Hot Tips

1. When finding a product on Click bank, it is recommended to filter these products via gravity. Aim to select products that are no less than 50 gravity score, as anything less than 50 means it probably isn't selling that well.

2. When using YouTube, put your affiliate links in the first 3 lines of your description. Also add it as a pinned comment on each video, so that it will always be on top. You want to ensure that these links can easily be seen by the buyer.

3. Save time and money on content creation by linking to the blogs, webinars, video tutorials, tools, and automated funnels developed by Shopify themselves for your audience.

4. There is a software package called AmaSuite which can automate the research part for you. You simply enter a list of criteria, such as "must be priced over £50 and have 100+ reviews", into the software. It will then return an extensive list of products which match your criteria. The software is able to produce extra data like the keywords people are using on Amazon to search for the products they want.

"The moment you make passive income and portfolio income a part of your life, your life will change. Those words will become flesh."

- Robert Kiyosaki

Plenty Of Swipes

With the increasing use of the Internet as a way for people to communicate, online dating sites such as Tinder, POF (Plenty Of Fish), Hinge and Match.com have become a highly popular way for single people to find romantic partners. The days of meeting someone special at work, cafes or a friend's party are gone. The world has never been so connected as it is now. It's the Internet that connects people when the lack of time and dynamic pace of life push them away from each other. In the world of gadgets, it isn't necessary to hunt for your soulmate, even for a short-term relationship, in a bar or club and long gone are the days when Internet dating was seen as a no-go. Now it's about as normal as Internet banking.

The online dating industry is a $2.3 billion business, with niche dating sites claiming more and more of that market share each day. It is easier than ever before to start a dating website; you do not need to be a programmer or design professional; you can outsource for that. The hardest part is putting together a concept that will attract people as members.

It's all in the name

Be mindful that people need to remember the name of your Dating app. It should be short, catchy and associative so users will be able to hear it once and remember it forever. Word of mouth will also work since users will share the name of your app with their friends and family if it offers good value to your target audience.

Steps in creating your site and app

1. Study the functionality and design of various dating websites and their apps.
2. Analyse the main benefits and features before you start building a dating website/app.
3. Create the structure and design of your dating site/app,
4. Use the right tech stack to create the website and dating app. If you are not a developer, then use Upwork or Fiverr to find one. Scale DM, too, can help with this.
5. Include MVP features on your website and dating app,
6. Choose which type of monetization strategy you prefer for your app.
7. Submit to top marketplaces such as Apple App store as well as Google Play store.
8. Launch your website.

Costs

Assuming a developer is charging around £50 p/h, one could cost you somewhere between £1000 - £5000 for a dating website. Luckily there isn't much difference in iOS and Android app cost. A better way to breakdown price would be to show you an example in features.

- Social sign-in - £1000 (average)
- User profile - £2750 (average)
- Geolocation - £350 (average)
- Matching Algorithm - £4000 (average)
- Chat & Communication - £8000 (average)
- Push notifications - £750 (average)
- Swiping - £500 (average)
- Settings - £1000 (average)
- Admin panel - £1250 (average)

Dating sites require a lot of upfront work, but once you establish your niche user base, and market to your chosen audience, it pretty much takes care of itself.

Your idea needs to target a specific type of personality, demographic or something as simple as a local area.

A few niche ideas for dating sites:

- Dating site for Vegans
- Dating site for Music Lovers
- Dating site for Busy Business Men/Women
- Dating site for those in Civil Service
- Dating site for High-Net worth Entrepreneurs
- Dating site for people with a disability

- Dating site for Super Genius'
- Dating site for Outdoor Lovers
- Dating site for Tattoo Lovers

You can pique users' interest with a FREE 14-day trial that then switches to a monthly membership, or you can offer a free version of the site/app then charge premium membership fees to unlock certain key aspects of the website/app. People are used to having paid upgrade offers and in-app purchases with this type of service. This can include: unlocking more users in your area, or guaranteed top appearances in searches. E.g., see who has liked your profile picture or see who has the most likes that day.

Special Bonus

Have you downloaded your FREE (£29.99 Value) bonuses yet? This includes a special PDF guide about niches. If not head over to:
www.businessmarketingfinance.com/readers

Hot Tips:

1. Use Facebook ads to target singles in your niche and watch your customer base grow. When this customer base is established, you could have an app built for it and further collect revenue via more ads and in-app purchasing.

2. Within your marketing plan, you should have a customer loyalty program. A loyalty program is a

rewards program offered by a company to customers who frequently make purchases.

A dating site loyalty program may give your users free rewards, money off upgrades, or even advance released products.

3. Make sure your app has a social login feature. Long registration processes already seem like a prehistoric fact that cannot survive today. So, a sign-in feature is a must-have. Let users register using their Facebook, Instagram, Twitter or LinkedIn account and start looking for a soulmate. Moreover, social sign-in gives users an opportunity to share your app on social media.

"It's all in the mind, change your mindset, and it will change your life."

- Darryl James

Retirement Plans

In my opinion, annuities are ideal for those who are aged between 60 – 75 and want a guaranteed passive income stream. An Annuity is an insurance contract where one or two people go into an agreement with an insurer for a chosen period. In short, you are the investor and you hand over a lump-sum amount of money to an insurance company, they then pay you a set amount of money every month for the rest of your life.

Simply stated, an annuity is a financial product sold by insurance companies that will allow you to put aside money, have it increase each year without paying taxes, and then trigger a stream of future payments on a timetable you may control. Those payments are taxed as ordinary income.

The idea of guaranteed lifetime income is a very attractive prospect, and an annuity can convert your pension into a steady stream of capital for the rest of your life or a specified amount of time.

Many people like this effortless way of earning passive income, as for the investment, you will receive a certain amount of revenue by the insurance/annuity company during the chosen period. You have the option to receive annuity payments for a lifetime. The income that you will receive will contain both a return of principal and interest.

The minimum investment is usually £5,000 to £10,000. With the flexible-premium annuity, the annuity is funded with a series of payments. Depending how much you invest, the first payment can be quite small. The immediate annuity starts payments right after the annuity is funded.

For example, you invest a lump sum of £100,000 into an annuity. An insurance company may then give you £1,830 in monthly income for the rest of your life. As you can quickly calculate, within ten years you will have received more money from the annuity than if you had simply kept the £100,000 in a bank account. Plus, you get the added benefit of continuing to receive those payments for the rest of your life.

There are three types of annuities to consider:

  • **Fixed Annuity** – Will pay out a fixed rate of return on the money that you invested. The majority of people choose this as it offers a predictable and guaranteed income stream. No matter what the condition of the financial market is; with a fixed annuity you can always expect a steady income stream every month.

• **Variable Annuity** – Will pay out a variable rate of return on the invested money. Here, the revenue stream will be connected (in part) to the stock market, and it will have the potential to increase if the markets increase. Of course, this also means that it may have the consequence of decreasing if the markets fall. Variable annuities have administrative fees, as well as mortality and expense fees. Insurance companies charge these, which often run about 1.25% of your account's value, to cover the costs and risks of insuring your money. Surrender charges are common for both variable and fixed annuities.

• **Indexed Annuity** – It will pay out a rate of return on the lump sum money that you will invest that is tied to an economic index. In simple words, it is a combination of the fixed and variable annuity.

This is because you will receive a minimum guaranteed payment during most situations and a higher rate when the market does well.

Paying Tax
If you purchase an annuity with pre-tax currency, payments from the annuity will be fully taxable as income. If you buy an annuity with after-tax funds, you are required to pay taxes only on the earnings. One of the main tax advantages of annuities is they allow investments to grow tax-free until the funds are withdrawn

Hot Tips:

1. Insurers make money on annuity fees and management services. As they invest your annuity payments or premiums, they get to keep anything above the payments they have guaranteed to you.

2. Insurers get to keep any remaining funds in your annuity contract once you have passed away and after they have settled any remaining payment obligations to your heirs. This being said make sure you read any fine print.

"The key to financial freedom and great wealth is a person's ability or skill to convert earned income into passive income and portfolio income."

Robert Kiyosaki

Storage Rental Made Simple

The demand for self-storage facilities is bigger than ever. As homes grow smaller and small businesses store their stock, both personal and business storage are profitable. Self-storage facilities share the same attractive qualities as other similar commercial real estate investing niches such as residential rentals, apartments, office buildings, and industrial properties.

The cash-flow potential can be fantastic, but just like all real estate investment deals, it all comes down to the management and the control of your profit margins. Any errors made in self-storage investments, such as over-valuation, a lousy location, high vacancy rates, are going to be far more detrimental to your bottom-line than residential. Owning a self-storage business can be very lucrative. Simply put, you are responsible for the personal property of your customers.

Self-storage is a fast-growing sector of small businesses and real estate. Examples of this could be self-storage unit companies such as Big Yellow Box and Storage Base here in the UK. People will always need a place to store their things. If you own land and it's not in an excellent location for a commercial business, develop it into storage units. For a small rental fee, every month people (especially non-resident students) will fill the storage units with their belongings.

You need to have a clear picture of the local demand, the local competition and the kind of costs and profits you might be looking at. Looking at sites such as Big Yellow Storage and Storage Base in the UK can give you a good idea of price/space ratios, etc.

The typical self-storage investment model usually involves an operator securing the freehold or leasehold of a property, then developing and finally opening and operating a storage centre. Depending on where you live, storage facilities vary in size and can range from a handful of units to over 1000 units in some of the largest locations.

Typically, a self-storage facility makes a profit at 60% to 70% of full occupancy. Currently, the industry average occupancy stands near 90%, according to Statista.

The essential part of any self-storage business is the actual location where your customers will store their items. Obtaining a secure space for storage in an area that is accessible should be your first significant expense.

Look for somewhere that has a lot of traffic and is correctly zoned for business development.

The self-storage industry can be very competitive. The number and quality of competing operators in a market area will have a huge impact on the rents and occupancy of a facility. The main barrier to entry is the capital costs in acquiring the real estate and developing the store. While this is significant, it has not prevented self-storage becoming oversupplied in some areas.

Don't limit your online presence to just your website. Self-storage directories get a lot of traffic and can help when people are searching for results.

Word of mouth is always the right way to go with this type of industry, so make sure you create an excellent customer experience.

When your self-storage is up and running with good profits, you may consider expanding it. This might involve increasing the number of storage units or obtaining land and building another self-storage with the same branding across town.

Overall this income stream has the following benefits:

- Huge upsell opportunities
- Increasing demand
- Low operating costs
- Ease of Financing
- Low risk
- No Need for repairs

Self-Storage Operating Costs are much lower than you may think. Self-Storage Investments loan default rates are significantly lower (banks like this).
There are many ways to profit – selling padlocks, empty cardboard boxes, & moving supplies, van rentals, etc.
The Manager of your storage business will have a major impact on the occupancy or particular storage units or sizes. Their level of training and sales skills are critical in this regard.

Any passive investor in the industry should ensure that their investment arrangement has a method of monitoring management performance to agreed objectives and appropriate actions for under (or over) achieving these goals. I remember needing to use a local storage unit for a few months many years ago and the manager was so rude I ended up moving my items to a storage unit many more miles away. So be careful who you leave running your new storage unit empire!

Hot Tips:

1. This can be a very low maintenance passive income idea. As long as each storage unit has its own key, the whole operation will be self-service.

2. Ask your solicitor about the various grants and financial aid schemes that exist for small businesses to determine if you are eligible for financial support from the government - remember work smart, not hard!

"Remember success is not what you have done compared to what others have done - it is what you have done in comparison to what you could've done."

- Tony Robbins

Recruitment Agency Lessons

As the demand for niche services is on the rise, many people are starting their own recruitment businesses and make big money from this from the comfort of their own home, hot desking or just a small office they rent.

Temporary worker agencies or staffing services, as they are sometimes called, find staff for business and vacancies for people who need them. The agency interviews and screens applicants for work placement. The goal of a recruiting agency may be to fill temporary job openings, permanent vacancies or both.

Once someone gets a job through the recruitment agency, the recruitment agency acts as a middleman to lease out that person to the employer and collects a fee on top of what is billed for that person's hourly wage.

For example, let's say one of my client projects for my digital marketing agency, Scale DM (as mentioned earlier), needs a freelance photographer. If I hire someone through a recruitment agency that focuses on creatives with a budget of £25 per hour, the agency finds me a freelance photographer, I pay the agency £25 per hour, and the agency staff is paid £20 per hour at a rate of 20% (£20 to the employee and £5 to the agency). As a recruitment agency, the more people you outsource, the more fees you can collect.

These 7 steps are what you need in order to start:

1. Business bank account
2. Accounting software or person
3. Legal requirements
4. Business insurance
5. Terms and conditions and contracts
6. A clean well-designed website for both recruiters and potential temporary workers
7. Engage where your audience is. This is usually on LinkedIn and Twitter, but other social media platforms could be useful for say chefs or the cooking industry.

LinkedIn for recruitment
LinkedIn describe their approach to business as "LinkedIn is much more than a social site. It's a community of professionals – in a business mindset – that's waiting to hear from you."

Many people might not be aware but a handy tool to use on LinkedIn for recruitment agencies is:

LinkedIn Recruiter – With it you can:

Find new people
Search for, connect with, and manage your top candidates in one place. With LinkedIn Recruiter you can gain access to the full member network and reach talent you won't find anywhere else. Use advanced search capabilities, smart suggestions, and spotlights to find the right candidates for your roles.

Post jobs
A hire is made every 10 seconds on LinkedIn. Job Slots give you the flexibility you need to fill roles as they open and reach the candidates you won't find anywhere else. And you can even attract top passive candidates via 'Jobs You May Be Interested In'.

Attract new clients
Showcase your company culture and make your employer brand stand out. LinkedIn Career Pages is a powerful employer branding tool that allows candidates to connect with your company, view open jobs, and gain insights into what it's like to work for the organisation.

The Industry-Standard Recruiting Tool | LinkedIn Talent Solutions
https://business.linkedin.com/talent-solutions/recruiter

The successful start of a recruiting agency involves having a concrete business plan, a background in recruitment strategies, knowledge of laws about licensing, hiring and taxes, and a marketing plan for gaining clients.
Be prepared to deal with continuous human resources management such as turnover, terminations, and disciplinary action when staff are late or do not turn up for work.

If you're placing contractors in a place of work, it's essential that your agency has the same insurance as the contractors themselves, so that liability can be passed down the line. Policies you should evaluate:

- Professional Indemnity insurance
- Public Liability insurance
- Employers' Liability insurance
- Cyber and data risks insurance

The most successful recruitment agencies focus on a niche. You will want to concentrate on having an agency recruiting a specific industry type only, such as teaching, administration, banking, or, like one of my previous clients, a recruitment agency in which she focused on the medical industry. This was a great idea and she has been very successful over the past 5 years.

Keep an up to date database of clients and candidates, making sure you follow the latest guidelines of data protection as well as GDPR (in the UK).

Make this truly passive by hiring a manager and staff to support your clients and candidates.

Essential elements of your website:

1. Make sure your website is user friendly and the colours match your brand,
2. Have nice clean images (preferably stock images from shutterstock.com or unsplash.com),
3. Make sure your Calls to Action are obvious – If your CTA is for the users to sign up, make that obvious in your content and clearly label as such,
4. How do people get in touch? Ensure your contact details are easy to find and your phone number is visible on each page. I recommend this being at the top of your header.
5. Make sure that you set your website address to auto-renew! The last thing you want is your website going down because the domain has run out!

Hot Tips:

1. Determine if a demand exists for your selected niche. If the market is already saturated, you might want to choose to change your niche, partner with an existing agency or open the business in a different geographic location.

2. Research laws related to advertising for employees. Become familiar with equal opportunity employment legislation and restrictions about how to avoid discriminatory practices in advertising job

openings. Determine if you must carry disability, unemployment or other types of insurance for your employees.

"What we are aware of, we can control and what we are unaware of controls us. Stop letting other people tell you how to spend the minutes of your day."

- Tony Robbins

Online Interview Boss

Usually used for recruitment, Online interviews are becoming more and more popular.

An online interview is an online research method conducted using computer-mediated communication (CMC), such as instant messaging, email, or video. Online interviews require different ethical considerations, sampling and rapport than the practices found in traditional face-to-face (F2F) interviews.

Source - Wikipedia

On demand online interviews are great. There are many industries they can work for and the process is quite simple. Line up a series of experts in a specific niche or industry, film using the latest smartphone camera or SLR, edit the interviews, brand them and offer people access to these interviews either via paid online subscription, or, if you've recorded just the audio, transform them into an audiobook.

Thankfully the digital age we are in today leveled the playing field, and almost anybody can be reached via social media or LinkedIn. Sometimes it only takes the guts to introduce yourself and reach out to them, of which you have, or you wouldn't be reading this book. You will be surprised how many experts despite time and status, will actually respond to you.

Tips for getting an interview with someone you admire:

Your elevator pitch
Speak about your experience, why you want to interview them (admiration, knowledgeable etc) and what you can also give to them.

Get in contact
Try using every angle to get their email, LinkedIn profile or PA/agent details. Usually, you can find this out by researching other interviews they have done. Conduct a search on LinkedIn or use websites such as www.Hunter.io

Be persistent.
Just because you've sent your pitch - but the request is now just seemingly wafting away in the great internet abyss un-replied - it doesn't mean it's a no. Follow up!

Let's say you love to cook, own a restaurant, or you are a budding new chef and want to put out a series where you interview chefs you admire and/or look up to in the industry such as Gordan Ramsey, Jamie Oliver or Marco Pierre. Do you want to ask them where they get their inspiration from? What happens when things go wrong in the kitchen? Or even worse, when the restaurant gets a bad review by a KPI (key person of influence) in media? These interviews will either be made into an audiobook or available as video via paid subscription on your website. First of all, do what I did, contact all the people you marvel at, all the gurus and experts you find intriguing and ask them if they wouldn't mind being interviewed for your website or audiobook. Tell them why you think they will be a good candidate for it.

You will then arrange a time to meet up, interview with a voice recorder or video and "sit at the feet" so to speak, of all these chefs. After you record their answers and the dialogue you shared, now it's time to sit down and edit either the recorded video clips or audio file. Granted some may say no, but what if they say yes?

Don't give up, work your way through your list and make each message personalised to the person you're writing to.

You will then have a wealth of knowledge you can use in your career or business and also have a new passive income stream.

Hot Tip:

When editing your video or audio recording, try to make it as professional as you can. If you don't have the skills either learn them via YouTube (simple search often will do) or hire someone to do it for you. Make sure you have top and tail branding too. Your paid subscribers should be reminded that it is your brand that has produced these awesome interviews.

"Strive not to be a success, but rather to be of value."

–Albert Einstein

Powerful Website Themes

Website themes are a great way of turning your web design by-products into some serious cash flow each month by selling them online. This can range from WordPress, Drupal, and Joomla themes, all the way to Magento and Shopify themes and, of course, HTML newsletters to be used with the likes of MailChimp.

A theme dictates the look and style of a website. A theme is made up of a range of things, such as font types and sizes, colour schemes and other areas that affect the aesthetics of a website. A theme helps reflect a brands identity through their site and helps improve user experience.

Businesses are always looking to give their website a fresh new look, and your theme could be just the thing they are looking for.

Chances are any website built before 2011 was created using HTML and very minimal (if any) elements of CSS or Java and possibly no CMS (content management system such as WordPress, Joomla or Drupal). This means that, if you create a theme for them to use, they can update many of the features themselves, which is a huge plus for a business or individual who has regular content to add. This way they don't have to either wait for their web developer to have free time in their schedule. or pay the cost each time to do so.

WordPress themes are selling at a tremendous rate right now, so they are very popular and profitable. Thousands of web designer/developers are making anywhere from £500 to £30,000 a month by selling their website themes online.

That being said, the market is quickly becoming oversaturated so you will need to bring something new to the table to entice buyers. The good news is that, if you have a great theme that you first mocked up the design for, you can always release it as a PSD and HTML version of it as well.

Tips for getting started using WordPress

- **Choose a niche** - you want to create a template that is targeted at a specific group of people. This can be cupcake makers, furniture stores, spa owners etc.
- **These types of themes** tend to sell the best, as the buyer can then use the same backgrounds and images you used for your demo of the theme.

- **Explore existing themes first** – learn what the competition is doing and read reviews to see what actually works.
- **Choose your framework -** you need to decide whether you are going to build your WordPress theme from scratch or customise an existing template.

- **Hunt out some high-quality stock images** – These are for your themes page demos.
- **Don't forget plugins** – WordPress has an extensive list of plugins, some of the most popular plugins bundled in themes are:

  Yoast SEO: An SEO plugin for improving website visibility and search rankings.
  Contact Form 7: A customisable, flexible contact form.
  Akismet: A spam-fighting plugin to protect against comment and contact form spam.
  Jetpack: An all-in-one plugin for analytics, design, marketing and security.
  WP Rocket: Rocket fuel caching for speeding up WordPress and improving web traffic.

Truly consider the best possible way to organise your code and files for submission. A passing W3C score is excellent, but there is always a way to improve your code with better white-space usage, proper file naming, writing semantic markup, and finding fewer complex methods of writing frequently used markup or scripts.

Consider your customer's experience when thinking about the types of options you wish to include. You will enable them to tailor the website, so it is paramount that you make sure your theme submission is well documented. In the long run, it will also prevent any support disasters where people get confused about how something works.

One of the best places to sell your theme is ThemeForest. ThemeForest is a platform that allows you to buy and sell HTML templates as well as themes for popular CMS products like WordPress, Joomla and Drupal.
Once you pass their criteria and prove that you are able to help the customers who purchase your theme (they have features that enable you to reach their 3 million customer base) then you are ready to go.

Hot Tips:

1. If you are a good designer, but your developer coding skills are not up to par or vice versa, why not partner up?

2. Keep in mind that the more work you can do yourself, the more control you will have, and the more money will stay in your pocket.

3. Above all ,create a theme that you, yourself would buy!

"You can never cross the ocean until you have the courage to lose sight of the shore."

–Christopher Columbus

Podcast Toolbox

Podcasting is a great way to express your passion about a particular subject, interest or to share information, knowledge or wisdom. As I have a passion for all things Business, Marketing and Finance (personal finance), I launched my podcast channel in April 2019 with the exact same name "Business Marketing Finance". My podcast spotlights today's most exciting and inspiring Entrepreneurs, marketing professionals, and business owners out there. The BMF podcast is currently on all podcast platforms (Apple, Google, Spotify plus 8 other platforms) and since its launch, it has a growing weekly audience of 922 subscribers across 15 countries around the world including, UK, USA, UAE, Vietnam, Singapore, Canada, Iran and the list goes on. I have already interviewed the likes of Daniel Priestly (Dent Global), Adam Field (Chelsea FC) & Robin Fisher Roffer (Big Fish Marketing) to name a few. My mission is to provide motivation and direction to my listeners, encouraging their entrepreneurial leap and helping them on their journey.

It is true that many people like to consume video content, however, audio podcasting retains a few advantages over video. First, people who drive are not able to watch video. Second, it is smaller in file size and can therefore be downloaded onto a phone or tablet, to be continued offline without taking up too much space.

When you are just starting out, to get your podcast on the platforms mentioned above and to make it easier for people to access your new show, I recommend using **Anchor FM.**

Anchor FM is a free podcasting platform that makes creation and distribution of your podcasts really easy in just 3 simple steps.

1. You sign up for free
2. You grow your audience
3. Anchor FM runs advertisements at the start and end of your content to pay for the bandwidth

Do I need RSS?
Don't worry if you are Unfamiliar with RSS. They offer a one-click distribution service. Anchor FM easily distributes your podcast to every major podcast platform, including:

- Spotify
- Apple Podcasts
- Breaker

- Castbox
- Google Podcasts
- Overcast
- Pocket Casts
- Radio Public.

All it takes from you is one click; and they handle everything else.

Anchor FM is set up to be a one-stop shop for podcasting. In Anchor FM, you can do all your recording, editing, analytics, and hosting, either via the free phone app, or online at Anchor.fm. Their mission is to democratise the audio. They believe everyone should be able to have their voice heard, regardless of background or experience level. Their aim is to make podcasting easy and fun, without sacrificing the quality every podcaster deserves.

As your podcast grows and has a large enough audience, you can receive income in the form of sponsorships and product mentions. On your show you can promote other people's products and services, and you'll earn a commission for doing so.
Many podcasting platforms do the work of matching you with great brands who are interested in sponsoring your show. You get to decide which brands you want to work with, which episodes you want to monetise, and where in your episodes you want your ads to appear. All Sponsorships ads are read out by you, so you can blend them seamlessly into your show. Then, get paid whenever people tune in!

As reported by The Atlantic, popular podcasters can command from advertisers approximately $25 to $40 for every 1,000 listeners. Advertise Cast places the 2019 average podcast advertising rates throughout the industry at $18 CPM (cost per 1,000 listeners) for a 30-second ad, and at $25 CPM for a 60-second ad.

When selecting the topic of your podcast there are two directions you can go; you can go for a mass market audience or you can go with a narrow niche audience. It is important to mention here that consistency is crucial to your audience in order to keep your listeners engaged and make them wish to consume your next episode. So, stick to the plan, theme and topic.

Special Bonus

Have you downloaded your FREE (£29.99 Value) bonuses yet? This includes a special PDF guide about niches.
If not head over to:
www.businessmarketingfinance.com/readers

Hot Tips:

1. Other paid podcast platforms allow you to add three categories for Apple Podcasts. Anchor FM currently only allows one category. So, instead of being listed in Business, Health, and Science, your show will just be listed in one.

2. Why not try adding some flare to your podcast show by recording a special intro with music and sound effects? It will do wonders for your show!

"You miss 100% of the shots you don't take."

–Wayne Gretzky

P2P Lending

Unfortunately, in the UK Banks don't like to lend money out of the goodness of their hearts. They only lend when it is profitable. This is a positive for you, the investor, as it means you can get in on some of that action through peer to peer lending. Peer to peer lending matches those who need to borrow money with those who have money to lend.

The benefit for the borrowers is that they often don't qualify for traditional loans from banks or have poor credit. For the lenders, the interest they get on the loans can be higher than that of more conventional investments, sometimes averaging above 10%.

Most people never do anything with their money other than earning it, putting it into a bank account, and spending it. Although most people probably wouldn't think of it as traditional investing, peer-to-peer (P2P) lending could be thought of as such because YOU get to be the bank.

Thanks to the internet phenomenon that has become known to many as "crowd lending," the days of having to go to a bank to get the money you need for your small personal loan are long gone. All you have to do now is go online, create a profile, and wait for other people to fund what you're asking for.

The loan can be for anything: a business start-up, getting out of debt, a new car, etc. Once this person signs up to a peer to peer lending site and asks for a loan, they become the "borrower."

You the "investor" basically acts as a bank. You will sponsor the loans with your money - just like a bank. With this type of service, you lend the money and decide what interest rate you want to charge.

The interest rate of the loan will depend on the borrower's credit rating. Example:

   • Borrowers with good credit will pay the lowest interest rates (usually around 8%).
   • For borrowers with bad credit, the interest rate that must be paid is higher (sometimes over 30%).

The negatives are that the borrowers could default on their loans, but as long as you thoroughly review your candidates before you lend the money, then you should be fine.

Many sites are stringent with their process, but it is paramount for an investor to pay attention to the credit rating of the borrower. Peer to peer lending websites also perform credit checks on prospective borrowers and do any chasing for repayments on your behalf. This will decrease the risk of the borrower defaulting on their repayments.

Borrowers with good credit may produce the lowest returns, but they have the highest probability of paying back their loans in full. Investors with poor credit have the highest chance of failing to meet the obligations of their loans.

Since its inception, peer to peer investing has been quoted as producing anywhere between 6% and 12% returns! Compared to the 10% average growth rate of stocks, P2P investing isn't as bad of an investment.

Great Sites to take a look at are: Zopa, lending works and Ratesetter.

My recommendation however (no affiliation) is Twino, some of the benefits of using Twino are:

A Proven track record
TWINO has played a crucial role in the rapid expansion of P2P lending throughout Continental Europe – They have already originated over €1 billion in unsecured consumer loans since their inception in 2009.

Buy back guarantee

TWINO will buy back the loan (principal amount and accrued interest for full term), if a borrower is late with the repayment for over 60 days.

No currency risk
TWINO offers investments in EUR and GBP, to protect investors from currency risk.

Peer-to-peer lending is not saving – it's somewhere in between saving and investing.

Hot Tips:

1. Reducing Risk: Investors who do peer to peer lending usually use a simple strategy to lower the risk, and that is simply to diversify the number of investments to be made.
   For example, if a borrower needs £10,000, they will not receive the entire £10,000 from just one investor. The money for that loan will come from many investors in the form of £20, £50, and even £100 increments (called notes). By spreading their notes across many different borrowers, P2P investors can minimise the risk of default.

2. Don't invest a large amount of money in one loan because if it defaults, then your ROI is shot. The minimum amount you can usually lend is £25 so 100 loans at this price means £2,500. It's probably fine to start at £500 and increase it to £2,500 over

time. The bad news is, not everyone can participate in peer to peer lending.

3. Do your research!!!

"The most difficult thing is the decision to act, the rest is merely tenacity."

– Amelia Earhart

Sweat It Out

The fitness landscape has changed with specialised fitness studios increasing in popularity. High-end gyms and studios make up over 35% of the multibillion-dollar fitness industry. Exercise is not only about weight loss or building muscle mass - having stability and strength in your everyday routine is just as important. 24-hour gyms seem to be popping up and offering memberships at ridiculously low rates these days, sometimes as low as £9.99 per month. Nowadays, people want a whole buffet of options to choose from at a time that is convenient for them. Many of the gyms today offer a fully immersive fitness studio and functional training zone, Olympic lifting platforms, MMA area, free weights area, cardio/fixed resistance machines, spacious changing rooms with secure lockers and vanity stations.

As an active member of one of the trendsetters in the UK, you never actually notice that the gym you are using is simply a building with equipment, pretty much unmanaged. How are they able to offer that? Simple: It's nothing more than a rented building with exercise equipment inside. We the users of the gym come and go as we please.

You may feel quite confident in starting the business from the ground up with little to no outside support. Depending upon your experience, this is an exciting approach as you will have the freedom and flexibility to offer whatever you would like inside of your gym and own the rights to your business. If you get enough people to sign up, you could surpass your operational costs and make a considerable profit.

Do your research
As well as having a business plan, when opening a gym, demographics (check the latest census) are vital. For example, if the area you are opening in has a median resident age of 50, the population is over 60% female, and the estimated median household income is £25,000 it may not be the best idea to specialise in Mixed Martial Arts that focus on grappling holds and takedowns.

Startup or Franchise?
If you want total freedom and want to make every business decision yourself, then a startup is for you. If you're starting from scratch, however, creating a strong brand and minimising startup costs may become a challenge so I would advise purchasing a franchise if branding and awareness may be an issue. When you buy into a fitness franchise, a lot of the work has already been done for you in terms of building a brand and creating a blueprint for success. Sometimes you will need to budget

for monthly royalties on top of an annual franchise fee in your business plan. So, be aware of that.

Financing

As well as licenses and permits, gym equipment leasing, legal fees and insurance, don't forget to include gym management software and hardware to your cost estimations. When planning your finances, look at your overall costs as well as monthly payments. Hidden fees can always pop up, so make sure to have some financial cushioning in place for this.

Legal

When it comes to business insurance, make sure you have adequate cover in place to protect you from any insurance claims. No matter how well-worded your policies and legal contracts are, if any client hurts themselves due to faulty gym equipment, a claim could be made.

Marketing & Advertising

All businesses need to have marketing to get the word out. This stream is no different. In today's digital age, marketing comes down to building an online following presence. Social media marketing and advertising are essential.

Whether it's Facebook/Instagram ads, connecting with a well-known fitness influencer (maybe one of the PTs you bring on board can become one) or regularly sharing "behind the scenes" snippets through Instagram stories, there are numerous different ways to market your new business venture.

Free Trials

When a new gym opens, potential members don't want to feel like they're being pressured to get a gym membership just for being curious. Offering free trials with no strings attached will get people to try your gym risk-free without feeling pressured. During this trial you can get valuable data and contact information. So, even if they don't sign up for a monthly membership, you can still market your latest offers, fitness classes, equipment upgrades and more.

Hot Tips:

1. Invest in a high-security camera system and have enough liability insurance, since injuries at the gym can be somewhat frequent if the user has not had a proper induction. You cannot stop anyone from coming in to train at 4 am after a night out, when there is a much higher risk when using the gym equipment. But you can minimize the risk.

2. Leasing your gym equipment from the manufacturer or a third party with a maintenance package is a great option when opening up a gym.

3. Whether you are leasing to own or utilising a residual lease, make sure your lease is with a fitness equipment manufacturer whose equipment holds a high resale value. Also, it is important that they have spare parts readily available, as gym equipment is prone to wear and tear.

Conclusion

"Only through growing pains do you become whom you were destined to be" Darryl James.

I appreciate you taking the time to read this book, and I hope it has given you practical ideas on some of the different ways to go about building residual income for yourself. I hope you feel more empowered to **take action**. By taking a hard look at your thought patterns and identifying the areas that may need improvement, I believe you are taking the first steps to getting out of the rat race.

You do not have to make millions of pounds. You can make as much as you like, that is the beautiful thing about passive income. Earn enough to travel the world like a king or make enough to cover your current lifestyle and become financially free. The choice is ultimately yours - follow your own bliss.

When I started writing the third edition of this book, I asked myself the following question:

"How can the book I am about to rewrite add more value and help even more people?"
I genuinely want to see people live life on their own terms, pursuing their dreams freely.

It is my desire to help you become your own boss, to help you contribute your gifts to this world, discover your life's purpose and have more free time to spend with your loved ones.

Be careful whom you associate yourself with, as my mentor told me. "If you want to become a millionaire start hanging around with millionaires."

It is important to ask yourself the question "Are my friends empowering me or disempowering me?" It's a tough question but in order to go to that next level, some people will have to stay in your heart and not in your life.

If you bought this book on Amazon, Barnes & Noble, Google or any other marketplace, and liked it or found it useful, I would really appreciate if you could kindly rate it 5 stars. It helps these platforms to better market this book, and more reviews mean more people that I can reach and help.

You now have the 30 Passive income streams that I recommend everyone to consider in order to build their passive income portfolio and become financially free. If you are interested in my new passive income course, more in-depth and over the shoulder type of training; if you'd like to "level up" the results from this book, then head over to www.businessmarketingfinance.com for strategies, tips, and even more resources.

If you would like to attend our next live event, where I and other entrepreneurs and millionaire investors share ideas, industry secrets and our thoughts/tips on passive income and investing, then please sign up using the address below.

www.businessmarketingfinance.com/passiveincomeevent

Whether it's your money or your time, Happy Investing!

Darryl James

Darryl James' next book is called ...

"Income Generating Assets" - How to ensure everything you touch, you own a piece of.

Notes

Useful Terms

ROI - Return On Investment

Capital Gains - A capital gain is a profit that results from a sale of a capital asset, such as stock, bond or real estate, where the sale price exceeds the purchase price.

Hedge Fund - An offshore investment fund, typically formed as a private limited partnership, that engages in speculation using credit or borrowed capital.

Diversify your Portfolio - When you diversify, you aim to manage your risk by spreading out your investments.

Bonds - When you invest in a bond, you are essentially loaning money to a company or government. Provided that nothing bad happens, like bankruptcy, you can cash in the bond on the maturity date and collect the interest.

Stocks - When you buy stock in a company, you are purchasing a tiny bit of ownership in the firm. Generally, the better the company performs, the more your share of stock is worth. If the company does not do so well, your stock may be worth less.

Mutual Fund - In layman's terms, this is a pile of money that comes from many investors like you and is then invested in assets like stocks and bonds. A mutual fund may hold hundreds of stocks, with the purpose of spreading the risk. In most cases, money managers make, buy and sell decisions for mutual funds, which brings us to our next definition.

Target-date fund - Often found in 401(k) plans, target-date funds are designed to serve as all-in-one portfolios that are tailored to your expected retirement date. So, if you have about 30 years until retirement, you might invest in a 2045 target-date fund. In the beginning, your investments will be riskier and more heavily weighted toward stocks, then as you get closer to 2045, the investments will become increasingly more conservative and will shift to include more bonds.

Annual report – The formal financial statement issued yearly by a corporation. The annual report shows assets, liabilities, revenues, expenses and earnings, how the company stood at the close of the business year, how its fared profit-wise during the year, as well as other information of interest to shareowners.

Assets – Everything a corporation owns or that is due to it: cash, investments, money due it, materials and inventories, which are called current assets; buildings and machinery, which are known as fixed assets; and patents and goodwill, called intangible assets.

Liabilities – All the claims against a corporation. Liabilities include accounts, wages and salaries payable; dividends declared payable; accrued taxes payable; and fixed or long-term liabilities, such as mortgage bonds, debentures, and bank loans.

Blue chip – A company known nationally for the quality and wide acceptance of its products or services, and for its ability to make money and pay dividends.

Cash flow – Reported net income of a corporation plus amounts charged off for depreciation, depletion, amortisation, and extraordinary charges to reserves, which are bookkeeping deductions and not paid out in actual dollars and cents.

Equity – The ownership interest of common and preferred stockholders in a company. Also, refers to an excess of the value of securities over the debit balance in a margin account.

Investment – The use of money for the purpose of making more money, to gain income, increase capital, or both.

Liquidity – The ability of the market in a particular security to absorb a reasonable amount of buying or selling at affordable price changes. Liquidity is one of the most important characteristics of a good market.

Stock exchange – An organised marketplace for securities featured by the centralization of supply and demand for the transaction of orders by member brokers for institutional and individual investors.

ABOUT THE AUTHOR

 Darryl James has been on his entrepreneurial journey since he was 29. He is a best-selling author, speaker and successful entrepreneur based in Birmingham, England.

Darryl is a student of life; he believes "The day you stop learning", is the day you stop earning". Darryl loves to travel and is the host of weekly podcast series Business Marketing Finance. He is the CEO of Scale DM, BMF, DMJ Publishing and Our Time Music as well as an international artist/music producer and enjoys a nice Cognac on the rocks.

Through his Business Marketing Finance website (www.businessmarketingfinance.com), Darryl helps entrepreneurs and authors with business strategy, entrepreneurial creativity, writing, publishing, and digital marketing. BMF is regularly voted as one of the top sites for entrepreneurs and self-publishers. Darryl has a popular podcast, Business Marketing Finance, on nine platforms including iTunes Spotify & Google Play, where he interviews key persons of influence, high-level entrepreneurs and CEOs.

Darryl's mission is to inspire and give those that need to excel the tools they need to create the future they know is possible. He believes NOW IS the time to turn your brilliant ideas into reality.

Printed in Great Britain
by Amazon